"A parent who has been there and a compassionate doctor combine to create a winning combination of practical assistance and compassion. I recommend this book to any parent who wants to learn more about taking care of their child with autism—and themselves."

> —Ken Duckworth, MD, medical director at National Alliance on Mental Illness and assistant clinical professor at Harvard Medical School

"Finally, a book for parents of children newly diagnosed with autism that's accurate and practical without being intimidating or alarmist. This how-to guide will help parents focus their energy and efforts so that their child benefits. I wish I'd had this introduction to autism when my daughter was first diagnosed."

> —Alison Singer, president of the Autism Science Foundation

"Feeling overwhelmed and confused about what to do to help your autistic child? Help awaits you with this book, an authoritative yet deeply empathetic and highly practical guide to navigating the challenging terrain of autism, from getting a diagnosis to choosing the right therapy. I wish my wife and I had had such an enormously useful primer when my son was diagnosed with autism in the late 1990s. It would have been our bible, like *What to Expect When You're Expecting* is for pregnancy. The authors have done parents of children with autism a huge service with this book, which, above all, offers a truly hopeful way forward."

> —Peter Tyson, father of a fifteen-year-old autistic boy

D0094231

"As indicated by its subtitle, this book is not a how-to manual, nor is it a book that advocates one view or another regarding this very complex disorder known as autism. The authors have presented a guide for parents, families, and caregivers with regard to understanding what is and is not known about the disorder, evaluating the strengths and weaknesses of the child, establishing medical and educational teams to best support the needs of the child and the family, becoming an effective advocate for the child, handling potential family stresses, and negotiating a multiplicity of interventions and treatment options. This book is well-researched and exceptionally well-balanced in its approach and is a thoughtful, common-sense guide to setting reasonable expectations and successfully negotiating the world of the autistic child."

> —Margaret L. Bauman, MD, associate professor of neurology at the Harvard Medical School, director of the Autism Research Foundation and the Autism Research Consortium, and founding director of the Lurie Center for Autism

"With the assurance and steadfastness of a Sherpa climbing Mt. Everest, Sastry and Aguirre expertly guide parents through the process of learning, providing intervention for, educating, and ultimately understanding their child on the autism spectrum. This is a must-have for every parent, educator, and medical professional supporting individuals with autism."

> —Stephen M. Shore, EdD, assistant professor of special education

"This book is highly readable and makes the complexity of autism highly accessible to parents, who have an urgent need to know how to help their child. The authors bring to the book their invaluable mix of first-hand and professional experience."

> —Simon Baron-Cohen, FBA, professor of developmental psychopathology at Cambridge University and director of its Autism Research Centre

BOOK SOLD
NO LONGER R H.P.L.
PROPERTY

"A refreshing, parent-centered approach that empowers parents to go with their gut feeling while also providing realistic advice that promotes critical thinking. This book is an inclusive guidebook with practical notes for parents at all stages of the autism diagnosis."

> —Lisa Borges, executive director of the Doug Flutie, Jr. Foundation for Autism, Inc.

RICHMOND HILL
PUBLIC LIBRARY

AUG 0 9 2012

CENTRAL LIBRARY
905-884-9288

"This wonderful book will bring comfort and practical help to many families as they search for creative ways to relieve their children's distress, develop new skills, and find areas of joy. The biggest gift that Anjali M. Sastry and Blaise Aguirre offer is that their shared wisdom will spare some parents from the painful and slow trial-and-error process of sifting through the sea of options they encounter on the Internet. Their book is deeply respectful of every parent as the true expert on their own unique child's strengths, interests, and challenges. It is also uniquely thoughtful about mindfulness and other ways that parents can sustain themselves along the journey. This is an important addition to the family literature on autism spectrum disorders."

> —Joseph Gold, MD, chief medical officer at McLean Hospital

"*Parenting Your Child with Autism* is a guide to managing your life and family when you have a child on the autistic spectrum. This is not a book of answers, but a book of methods and processes. Sastry and Aguirre teach you how to find the help you need, how to manage all the meetings with doctors and educators, and how to evaluate all the conflicting opinions and recommendations. Most importantly, they teach you how to do the best for your child."

—Brian G. R. Hughes, parent, entrepreneur, and university trustee

"This book is a user-friendly, insightful, and practical guide for parents of children with autism. It empowers parents to take a leading role as an expert in their child's care and to bring their invaluable expertise as the primary care providers to the table. I highly recommend this book and believe that it will be of enormous benefit to children with autism and their families."

—Roya Ostovar, PhD, author of *The Ultimate Guide to Sensory Processing Disorder*

"As a lay person who has both worked with adolescents for over thirty-five years and is an aunt to a nephew with Asperger's syndrome, I found this book captivating. The simple (without being simplistic) explanations of the autism spectrum and the practical guides to coping left me feeling empowered. The mystery of autism was swept away and, in its place, I was left with a feeling of hope. Although there is currently no cure for autism, Sastry and Aguirre are encouraging with their advice. They assure caregivers of children with ASD that they can significantly improve the quality of life of those affected by autism. A very practical and optimistic read."

—Linda Schuyler, cocreator and executive producer of the award-winning *Degrassi* television franchise

Parenting Your Child *with* Autism

Practical Solutions,
Strategies, and Advice
for Helping Your Family

ANJALI SASTRY
BLAISE AGUIRRE, MD

New Harbinger Publications, Inc.

Publisher's Note

Care has been taken to confirm the accuracy of the information presented and to describe generally accepted practices. However, the authors, editors, and publisher are not responsible for errors or omissions or for any consequences from application of the information in this book and make no warranty, express or implied, with respect to the contents of the publication.

The authors, editors, and publisher have exerted every effort to ensure that any drug selection set forth in this text is in accordance with current recommendations and practice at the time of publication. However, in view of ongoing research, changes in government regulations, and the constant flow of information relating to drug therapy and drug reactions, the reader is urged to check the package insert for each drug for any change in indications and dosage and for added warnings and precautions. This is particularly important when the recommended agent is a new or infrequently employed drug.

Some drugs and medical devices presented in this publication may have Food and Drug Administration (FDA) clearance for limited use in restricted research settings. It is the responsibility of the health care provider to ascertain the FDA status of each drug or device planned for use in their clinical practice.

Distributed in Canada by Raincoast Books

Copyright © 2012 by M. Anjali Sastry and Blaise Aguirre
New Harbinger Publications, Inc.
5674 Shattuck Avenue
Oakland, CA 94609
www.newharbinger.com

Cover design by Amy Shoup; Text design by Michele Waters-Kermes; Acquired by Jess O'Brien; Edited by Nelda Street

All Rights Reserved

Printed in the United States of America

Library of Congress Cataloging in Publication Data on file

14   13   12

10   9   8   7   6   5   4   3   2   1

First printing

To my family. Life with Mark, Kiran, and Harry has blessed me with joy I could never have imagined and wisdom I could never have foreseen.

—Anjali

This book is dedicated to my children, who taught me how and how not to parent, and to Lauren, who put up with endless hours of edits and reedits.

—Blaise

RICHMOND HILL
PUBLIC LIBRARY

AUG 0 8 2012

CENTRAL LIBRARY
905-884-9288

Contents

Acknowledgments

Parents, children, teachers, therapists, and specialists shared their experiences, ideas, and insights with us in countless ways. Throughout our book, you'll find that we have learned much from others. Thank you to everyone who passed along a tip, told a story, sent an article, discussed a theory, or showed us how to do something. We are more grateful than we can express.

Our editorial team at New Harbinger cheered us on, helped us define our focus, and taught us that we could present this information in a way that is both evidence based and parent friendly. Special thanks go to Jess O'Brien for his relentlessly upbeat energy and to Nelda Street for her painstaking patience. And even before New Harbinger, there was our agent, Nancy Rosenfeld, whom we were glad to have at our side on this journey! As we completed the book we were grateful for Cara Cherson's professional and timely assistance.

Heartfelt thanks to cherished friends, family, and colleagues who read our drafts and offered us feedback and encouragement as we worked to develop our understanding of autism and parenting, and to find our voice as authors: Lauren Aguirre, Paul Asquith, Gauri Divan, Lisa Endlich, Josh Glenn, Joe Gold, Brian Hill, Irfan Ibrahim, Sarah Jean-Louis, Fiona Lee, Meghan Montgomery, Mark O'Brien, Shiba Nemat-Nasser, Joanne Oxley, Huggy Rao, Lois Sastry, Ram Sastry, John Sterman, Peter Tyson, and Rebecca Weintraub.

Introduction

You may not realize it, but you are a special kind of expert, and you're on your way to becoming even more of one. In the years to come, you will hone your understanding and skills. You and your family will benefit.

Like every parent, you're an expert on your own child. When your child has an autism spectrum disorder, you develop special kinds of expertise. Interactions with professionals, experiments with new approaches at home and school, family conversations about tough decisions, and your own observations and reflections build your knowledge and insight.

This is a book for parents, and here we are talking about experiments and working with professionals. Why can't you simply follow the instructions for parenting a child with autism? The problem is, there is no book that tells you how.

Walk into any well-stocked bookstore, and you'll find book after book on autism. They run the gamut from detailed scientific studies to compelling first-person narratives. In fields from genetics to education, more research than ever is tackling autism. But the journal articles and books fail to provide parents with the answers they most need. No matter how excellent the academic studies, they are not guides for what actions to take. Even if your background enables you to comprehend research papers (and you have the time to do so), how does it help you advocate for getting your child the right education?

And the personal accounts of others don't tell you how to meet the needs of your unique child in your specific circumstances. Parents know that the particulars matter, but they are not sure how to apply the information that's available. The vivid details of one family's journey out of autism may be inspiring, but even if you succeed in translating their experience into action steps, carrying them all out simply might not be feasible for you.

This is not to say that there's nothing practical out there: a growing collection of books teaches parents how to implement programs and techniques for everything from toilet training to social interaction. But you may still struggle with the strategic questions of what to try and what to drop. Not all interventions work. What advice should you follow to help your child? And can any book deliver on the promise of a cure?

Of course, books and studies provide invaluable information, and we make extensive use of them. But something else is needed.

Scientific Evidence Is Important but Falls Short

Families dealing with autism face crucial questions where scientific research meets practical strategy. The intersection of science and practice is not a place many parents plan to visit, and few are equipped to navigate its terrain. Road maps of this frontier territory are hard to come by.

This book is designed to help. We start by explaining why you need to combine research evidence with real-world experience.

Science continually influences how parents, teachers, and administrators think about autism and its treatment. This is part of a broader shift in medicine and education, toward what is known as "evidence-based approaches." To use evidence as your basis for selecting treatments, you choose only those approaches that are supported by the highest-quality research.

Now, we are all in favor of scientific evidence and draw on as much of it as possible in the pages to come. But when it comes to figuring out your child's issues and what could help, the formal evidence is often scant. And anyway, your kid is unique and may not respond as children in a clinical study did. How do you proceed to evaluate each potential treatment, therapy, teaching method, or cure, when nobody can predict what will work?

Not only do you need to look at each treatment option, but you also need to think of how everything fits together. Parents of children with autism wrestle with trade-offs, making choices amid limited information, constrained resources, and insufficient sleep. The published literature is of little help at these moments. There's a practical side to making parenting decisions that you cannot glean from reading all the research papers on autism.

Many fields, like behavioral psychology, art therapy, and executive function coaching, could contribute useful advice on parenting amid the kinds of challenges that autism poses, and we hope others will follow our call for more useful approaches that blend science and practice. Our book offers a starting point that places *you* at the center.

Parents Are at the Center

You already know that other parents are valuable sources of practical advice: they share tips in waiting rooms, distill personal experiences in blog posts, send e-mails through friends of friends, and answer all sorts of questions in online discussion groups. Much wisdom is contained in the parenting community, and we've been fortunate to tap into the insights and advice of others to complement our own experience.

But another family's experience or another parent's advice, no matter how compelling, is not scientific evidence. Parents can share great ideas for navigating medical and educational systems, getting by at school and in the community, and supporting your child's development. But to choose the right treatments, educational approaches, and developmental goals for your child, you need two more things. First, you need knowledge of your child's particular interests, strengths, and needs, along with a sense of what matters to your family. Second, to choose the best options, you need an understanding of the ideas that are supported by growing bodies of research and professional experience. And where the formal evidence falls short, you need to figure out what to do.

In such situations, you may assemble *your own* evidence. This involves gathering your own data, making sense of it, and combining it with other information. Equipped with these tools, you'll be able to evaluate whether your child functions better with a new treatment or a different teaching approach. Luckily, you won't have to go it alone. Your effort can enlist others, including the professionals who work with your child.

Admittedly, the situation is challenging. You face a lifetime of decisions about what's best for your child at a time when the science is uncertain and resources are limited. As you will see, autism spectrum disorders are complex. Every child and family is different.

Parenting a Child with Autism as a Journey

You might have to select classrooms and treatments in the coming months. You'll make numerous decisions about how to work with your child's teachers and therapists, your family, and the community, not to mention school authorities and health care providers. In addition, everyday life presents you with many choices about how to live with your child. What you do day to day also shapes your child's development.

This isn't news, of course. We parents know (even if we don't always act accordingly!) that our daily interactions with our offspring shape their behavior and learning. Let's say you want your typically developing kids to say "please" and "thank you." Use the right parenting strategy consistently, and eventually your kids will mind their Ps and Qs. But when your child has autism, routine parenting is not so easy, and every decision can seem weighty because you are working so hard to help your child learn without the advantage of the full complement of skills, capabilities, and motivation that drives development in typical children.

Making Many Decisions Means Having Many Chances to Learn

You'll be facing extra decisions, both big and small, as you choose how to live with, treat, and teach your child with autism. Perhaps you've already faced plenty of tough choices, and if the prospect of having to make more decisions seems daunting, take courage; it's *good* that there are many decisions ahead. You'll have multiple chances to learn, make course corrections, and come to terms with the complexity of the needs of your child and your family.

Chances are there's no single step that will set your child on the path to happiness, normalcy, and self-sufficiency. Maybe you've read about parents who rescued their child from autism with a special diet or therapy. We're here to tell you that the vast majority of children with autism are not cured by a single intervention. By itself, no dietary change, medication, or teaching curriculum will likely make your child look completely typical. Evidence shows that a combination of interventions and approaches over time help children with autism learn and develop. So, if you've picked up this book because you're facing a tough choice about what to do next, there's help for this decision and the next. We're here for the duration with a set of tools designed to help in a wide variety of situations. That's why we focus on the process or, to use a metaphor we'll return to, the journey. Parenting a child with autism may not be a journey many would choose, but as we hope to convey, good things come along with the challenges.

Even if the way forward seems difficult right now, it will get better. One day, you'll realize that life feels a little less arduous. If our book helps you get there any faster, we'll have reached our goal of helping to guide and ease your journey.

Why We Don't Instruct You on Specific Treatments

Our focus on the process and decisions means that we skip detailed instructions for implementing each option. We won't list every step in toilet training your child or explain how to teach her to read for meaning, although here and there, we'll go a little deeper if we think it helps convey a point. You can find instructions on specific interventions or programs elsewhere. These practical supports include workbooks, checklists, guides, tutorials and workshops, support groups, and discussion forums, along with experts and consultants you can turn to. We'll share some of these resources.

Our focus on *how* to choose means that we hold off on telling you *what* to choose. We are not proposing a particular method of teaching or treating a child with autism over other methods (unless we find evidence of potential harm or ineffectiveness in these methods). For most interventions, the jury's still out, for reasons we explain in some detail, but where we see promising results, we'll certainly mention it.

You are the decider. Our goal is to support your choice of which treatments and interventions to try. Once you try them, we'd like to help you figure out whether they actually work. So we would like to be part of your support team. The team's job is to coach you through the process of assessing, planning, and managing your child's treatment. Along the way we hope to help you realize what you are learning from the journey and value everything that makes your child and your family special.

What Went into This Book

Since we've invited ourselves onto your team, we think we should introduce ourselves and tell you about how we prepared the book, our stance on some important issues, and the readers we hope to reach.

The Authors

We represent two different roles: one of us is a parent of children on the autism spectrum and the other is a medical expert.

Anjali Sastry

As an MIT-trained academic in the field of system dynamics, I believe in the value of scientific research and embedding rigor and systematic thinking into my work. My professional experience in teaching management also equips me with practical insights and skills that complement Blaise's medical expertise. Perhaps my biggest—and most rewarding—management challenge has been parenting two sons who are on the autism spectrum.

My experience as a mother has made me the person I am today. I've learned firsthand the value of getting the right diagnosis, treatment, and interventions. I've come to value blending research with action, realizing that in order to have an impact, sometimes it's better to try something out and gather my own data instead of spending a lot of time reading reports and discussing hypotheticals. Many of the decisions that will confront my management students in their future careers also require action in the face of uncertainty and complexity, and I aim to teach them how to draw on research where useful and how to design their own experiments where it makes sense, just as I've done as a parent. I've redirected my professional work to take on the challenges of delivering health care in settings where resources are lowest and needs highest. In global health delivery, I continue to work on one of the themes running through this book: collaboration, management, field testing, and systems thinking can be marshaled to improve lives.

I've been lucky to combine my professional work with motherhood in a family that has forged its own path. Often, I am humbled by how much more I need to learn. It has been years since my older son was diagnosed with autism and my younger son with Asperger's disorder, but I'm no expert. I've learned much from my journey, but many mysteries remain.

My journey began at a point where you may be today: coming to terms with the diagnosis. It took too long—over a year—between our first inkling that something might be wrong with our oldest son and his formal diagnosis. Not until the summer after he turned three did my husband, Mark, and I learn officially that our older son was not developing in a typical fashion.

Of course, you know your child is unique from the moment you set eyes on him. But my sons' uniqueness has some special aspects. It's not always easy for others to recognize their challenges. It can be a source of annoyance or even shame. Perhaps, like me, you have been scolded by strangers for failure to control your child or have felt the sting of embarrassment when your kid did something weird at the mall. And along with worry about the future, I feel regret at the family events I've skipped over the years and the sleepovers my sons were not invited to. Families of typical kids take birthday parties and other events for granted, but they entail *so* much more effort and are *so very* much less fun for a parent like me.

I am still blindsided by the ferocity of my urge to fight for my sons when I see them treated unfairly. More often, now that it's been over a decade since we started this journey, I revel in the sweetest feelings of joy when my kids are happy. Our older son may not be much of a negotiator, and his planning is weak at best, but he does not scheme, manipulate, or ask us to buy him things. Running around the yard at dusk with the fireflies is, to him, more fun than playing with any video game, and I love him for showing his enjoyment of life in the most visible, physical forms of expression every day.

Life with our sons can present dramatic challenges. Safety can be a concern: our older son's extreme aversion to butterflies and dogs has caused him to bolt into traffic. Once, as we held hands in a park, he inadvertently pulled me down, and I injured my knee when he desperately tried to escape a butterfly I didn't even see. As a young child, he would attempt to injure himself. His behavior is sometimes subtly strange—for instance, when he stands a little too close to a stranger or uses unusual intonation in his speech.

Other challenges are more exasperating than anything: on hot summer days, it feels like we struggle daily with getting our younger son to wear anything besides long pants and a long-sleeved shirt or sandals with socks (which wouldn't be a big deal if he weren't prone to heat exhaustion). If we can get him into a polo shirt, it's impossible to get him to leave the top button undone. For him, feeling cool—or looking "cool"—clearly comes below other needs.

Our older son doesn't talk much. Sometimes I imagine a day when he'll explain everything to me, puzzling behaviors and all. But I've come to believe that it's not his job to account for himself. Rather, it's my job to support him. I've been cultivating my powers of observation and sense of curiosity, watching his behavior more carefully, looking for patterns and differences, jotting down notes, and planning what questions to ask his therapists and medical experts. Our interactions have changed, too. Now I ask fewer direct questions and instead make comments to draw his interest and spark his speech. This curiosity on my part reframes things I used to see as problems. In a sense, by trying to understand what I see my kids doing, I can be a bit of a scientist. This shift in approach enables me to test my assumptions, make discoveries, and flag my own and others' inappropriate assumptions. I also nurture my own empathy and appreciation of each child and realize how lucky I am to have them both in my life. And I hope the ideas we lay out in this book can do the same for you.

I have big ambitions for this book. Beyond the information and advice presented in its pages, I'd like to contribute to a larger conversation that connects us all: families, caregivers, therapists, experts, specialists, and people with autism.

Blaise Aguirre

My area of expertise is a psychiatric condition known as borderline personality disorder (BPD). I specialize in treating children, but why am I coauthoring a book on autism? The reasons are twofold. First, I have known Anjali and her husband, Mark, for many years. Their family has taught me more about the condition we call autism than my training ever did. Over the past decade and a half, we've shared ups and downs as parents, too, and it's wonderful to be able to connect our personal friendship with my professional experience working with children.

This brings me to my second point. BPD and autism share some interesting features. Both are developmental disorders. Those who share the lives of children who have these disorders struggle to understand their experiences and behaviors. People who have either condition have a hard time identifying and regulating their emotions.

Some may even turn to self-harm in response to experiences they cannot otherwise handle. People with autism struggle to read the emotions of others. People with BPD also misread others' emotions but often overrespond to what they interpret.

With every child I treat, I also work with the parents. My goal is to develop the parents' capacity to look at the world through their child's eyes. By imagining how their child experiences things, parents can make sense of their child's behavior. As parents, we can get stuck in our own perspectives, overlooking or discounting how others see the world. The tendency of parents to consider their own viewpoints as more valid than their child's can be a barrier to understanding and make both children and parents unhappy.

I believe that it is essential to strive for the most empirically valid, compassionate treatments available. I believe in moving away from the search for blame and fault, aiming instead to create the best lives possible for people with these conditions and all who love and care for them. In doing so, we empower ourselves to be better parents, caregivers, and human beings.

How We Prepared This Book

Our varied backgrounds and mutual interest in research shaped our aspiration to synthesize science and practice for parents who are dealing with autism. We reflected on our personal and professional experience, interviewed dozens of parents and experts, and conducted an extensive investigation of peer-reviewed journal articles. We cast a wide net to go beyond a merely formal investigation. Between the pair of us, we read hundreds of books, news stories, and web pages—not to mention a plethora of e-mail discussions, magazine articles, and blog postings. You are probably reading and learning from many sources too. We'll share some resources we've found useful, but because new knowledge of and approaches to autism are constantly emerging, a list will never be definitive.

The fact that knowledge will continue to accumulate shaped our goals for this book. Research will advance, teaching and interventions will evolve, and inspiring accounts of parents and people with autism will continue to emerge. Against this backdrop, we aim to equip you with a set of tools for making sense of ideas and options, both today and in the future. We designed our practical decision-making approaches to stand the test of time.

How We Chose Our Words

Because the topics addressed in this book are often complex, we'd like to explain the thinking behind some key terms and their implications for how we see the issues.

In writing this book, we have in mind a child whose diagnosis places her on the autism spectrum, but of course, your child is wonderfully unique, so you will need to adjust what you read according to your own child's needs and profile. In keeping with recent trends in expert opinion, we define the word "autism" broadly. The notion of the spectrum is helpful because it reminds us that autism is on a continuum and that there's fluidity: people can move along this spectrum as they develop. We avoid fine-grained distinctions within autism. You may encounter terms like "high functioning" and "low functioning," but with little clinical evidence for exactly where one type ends and the other begins, we prefer to focus on more general advice.

Although, throughout the book, we address "parents," we intend to include anyone involved in caring for and making decisions on behalf of a child with autism. You may be a single parent, part of a blended family, a grandparent, an older sibling, or some other caregiver.

Male and female pronouns are varied intentionally; we refer to your child as a son or as a daughter.

We call autism a condition, not a disease. Sometimes we label it "disability" or "impairment," but we also refer to it as a difference. The language matters because it's connected to the overall lens through which we see people who have autism, an issue we return to in our final chapter. Throughout the book, we tend to use phrases like "person with autism" (such *people-first language* emphasizes the person, not the condition). Within the autism community, there is a movement to reclaim the term "autistic," and we see great value in doing so. People-first language may soon be replaced, but for now, we tend to use it. Elsewhere we are less ambivalent: in referring to people who do not have autism, we avoid using the terms "healthy" and "normal," preferring instead "neurotypical" or "typically developing."

For reasons that we'll explain later, "intervention," "treatment," and "therapy" are used interchangeably, as is common practice. We use the term "medication" for medicines prescribed by licensed physicians. "Biomedical" refers to interventions that affect the body directly (such as supplements) but are not prescription medication.

The Reader We Hope To Reach

Over the years, friends, relatives, and acquaintances have asked us many questions about autism. Those phone calls and e-mails inspired us to write this book, and we aim to address you as fellow parents. Imagining you as someone whose child is in the process of being diagnosed, we built our chapters around the questions that are likely on your mind. How will you sort out what to do? You know that research and professional expertise are important, but you also know that you are the expert on your child. You know that you have to be practical above all else. And you are coming to terms with the fact that autism will, most likely, be a part of your life and your child's life forever.

A Quick Guide to This Book

Through the progression of chapters in this book, we aim to help you become the well-equipped, wise, and practical expert that your child needs you to be.

The first few chapters of this book build your understanding of autism spectrum disorders. We discuss definitions and a history of the diagnosis, sharing insights from people with autism. A survey of current thinking about causes and cures provides baseline knowledge for assessing potential treatments. An overview of common parenting challenges sets the stage for some advice designed to help you work through difficulties, now and in the future.

Next, we guide you through the practical aspects of getting a diagnosis, which will also aid in your ongoing efforts to build your understanding of your child's specific profile, partner with medical professionals, and select interventions that work. We then turn to a practical discussion of many alternatives you are likely to consider. An overview of medication and biomedical, sensory, and physical treatment options highlights evidence and ideas you'll find useful in making your decisions. We then develop a framework to inform our discussion of educational approaches and include practical advice for building an appropriate team. To round out our list of professional treatments, we consider specific approaches that target social interaction and language, two key areas of need.

The final essential ingredient for your child's learning and development is your family. To help you build an everyday life that works for your child with autism and other family members, we share suggestions that range from practical and educational to philosophical, closing with some personal and professional advice for your journey ahead.

Making It Useful: Practice Notes

To ensure that our advice can be put to practical use, we worked with parents and combed a variety of sources to distill experience into usable advice that relates to the topics at hand, framed as "Practice Notes." We incorporate these practical instructions and parent-tested suggestions throughout the book.

So now you have a sense of who we are, why we wrote this book, and the perspectives that inform our approach. We hope you find every chapter informative and instructive. And if we've accomplished what we set out to do, by the time you've reached the end of the book, you'll feel empowered and inspired too.

CHAPTER 1

What Is Autism?

People who see things differently have revolutionized art, science, and technology. Animal behavior expert Temple Grandin, who has autism, used her unusual visual skill and attention to detail to devise new ways of handling livestock. Her cost-effective and humane designs have made the world a better place. Grandin credits her teachers and family with helping her overcome the challenges of living with autism. Today, as an autism activist, she speaks to many people about her experiences, describing what it's like to think in pictures.

The tribe of people with autism includes Einstein, Mozart, and Tesla, Grandin (2010) tells us, hinting that some of today's technology innovators belong too. But not everyone with autism is a genius, and it doesn't seem right to expect everyone with the condition to offer a special talent that offsets his challenges. Many struggle to understand and get by in the world, but as we'll see, part of the challenge is the world's misunderstanding of people with autism.

We'll start with a broad picture of autism. To frame our discussion of its definition and diagnosis, we'll consider the path that society has taken to reach our current understanding, which is still incomplete and evolving. We close with a few sketches of the impact of autism on the lives of people who have the disorder.

Three Differences Define Autism

Experts talk about "the triad," three broad types of differences that define autism. The exact wording may vary, but they refer to impairments in the linked domains of social interaction, language and communication, and patterns of behavior.

Differences are often evident by the time a child with autism is a toddler, and they tend to persist as the child ages. Unlike other medical conditions, autism cannot yet be detected with a blood test or brain scan. Specialists look to specific behaviors in three areas to establish whether someone has autism.

- *Social interaction:* Broadly speaking, it's difficult for people on the autism spectrum to share experiences with others. Clinicians identify deficits in understanding other people's feelings and emotions.

- *Communication:* Difficulties in communicating range from an inability to produce meaningful words to problems making sense of and contextualizing what others say, write, or express nonverbally. A common problem for people on the autism spectrum is the inability to sustain typical conversation.

- *Interests and behaviors:* People with autism tend to exhibit behavior that others consider unusual or atypical. These behaviors can include curious and repetitive body movements or physical mannerisms, such as hand-flapping. People on the autism spectrum may also have narrow and intense interests.

A Brief History of How Autism Has Been Defined and Explained

Autism has suffered its share of misunderstanding and myth. The early 1800s saw the first written clinical descriptions of children who would be diagnosed with autism today. By 1911 the word "autism" was introduced by

Swiss psychiatrist Paul Bleuler to categorize people who had withdrawn from social interaction (in Feinstein 2010). Some of these patients would likely now be considered to have schizophrenia.

In 1943, Leo Kanner, the first psychiatrist to be identified as a *child* psychiatrist, published an investigation of autism. The article, "Autistic Disturbances of Affective Contact," was so influential that for a period, autism was referred to as "Kanner's syndrome." Kanner believed that the condition was due to a lack of maternal warmth and attachment to children, yielding the now-discredited "refrigerator mother" theory of autism.

In 1944, Austrian pediatrician Hans Asperger wrote "'Autistic Psychopathy' in Childhood." Both Kanner and Asperger differentiated autism from schizophrenia, noting that children with autism appeared to have had the condition since birth. Later, "Kanner's syndrome" was used as a diagnosis for children with more classical features of autism, while "Asperger's disorder" defined a category that included children with poor social skills but normal language ability.

In 1964 psychologist Bernard Rimland, himself a parent of a child with autism, challenged Kanner's explanation in the book *Infantile Autism: The Syndrome and Its Implications for a Neural Theory of Behavior.* For the first time, autism was presented as neurological in basis, caused by differences in the brain rather than by parenting.

The modern view emerged in 1979 in the United Kingdom, when physician Lorna Wing and psychologist Judith Gould studied a large sample of children with impaired capacities for reciprocal social interaction. They found that these children also had difficulties in communication and imagination, resulting in narrow, repetitive patterns of activities. Following their study, their concept of the linked "Triad of Impairments" spread, setting the stage for how we see autism today.

Recent Attention to Autism

Society's view of autism spectrum disorders, or ASDs, has shifted and likely will again. Our understanding of its origins will shift too. Autism has attracted growing attention, in part because of its enormous impact on society.

Increased Prevalence

The Centers for Disease Control and Prevention (CDC 2009) found that around 1 percent of all eight-year-old children in the United States met criteria for an ASD in 2006. That means that 40,000 eight-year-olds alone were affected. An ASD was found in 1 in 70 boys and 1 in 315 girls; boys are four to five times more likely to have the condition.

Between 1990 and 2002, the fraction of children diagnosed with an ASD grew by 600 percent. Careful studies attribute roughly one half of the recent increase in autism to better detection and diagnosis (Hertz-Piccotto 2011). The rest is the real increase: in just twelve years, the number of kids with autism jumped. The tripled prevalence means that three times the fraction of kids had autism in 2002, compared with just over a decade before. The CDC estimated 1 in 110 children in the United States to have the condition in 2011, and experts predict the prevalence will rise further.

Financial Cost

Another measure is the financial cost. Parents know all too well the high cost of raising a child with autism, but society pays a high price too. Harvard researcher Michael Ganz (2006; 2007) calculated lifetime-care costs for one person with autism to be *over $3.2 million*. Multiply that by the number of people with an ASD, and that's a staggering amount of health care dollars! Many sources indicate that beyond the United States, world-wide health care and education costs related to autism are expected to grow to unsustainable levels, an outcome that concerns public health officials, doctors, and government leaders. Clearly we need to understand more about causes and treatments, which is one reason so many families support autism research.

But although the societal impact of autism is important, we are concerned with the day-to-day lives of children who have this condition and their families. We'll focus on ASDs, but our approach to parenting applies to other conditions involving nontypical development, including fragile X syndrome, Rett's disorder, childhood disintegrative disorder, and tuberous sclerosis. All are neurodevelopmental conditions that share some features of autism.

Definition vs. Diagnosis

Parents need to know how autism is defined to ensure that they and the experts agree that they are looking at the same condition. When it comes to seeking diagnosis, some parents are understandably reluctant to see their young children labeled with a disorder like autism. What does it mean if your child doesn't behave like other children? It could help to know that there are various possible diagnoses. On the autism spectrum alone, terms you may hear include everything from "pervasive developmental disorder not otherwise specified" (PDD-NOS) to Asperger's disorder (also referred to as AS or Asperger's syndrome) and autism. The use of these terms is in the process of shifting again, as medical and allied professionals make sense of new findings, which is another reason it's important to work with your clinicians to understand how they apply the terms.

Parents may come to the diagnostic process reluctantly, but once there, many seek certainty in the label that is attached to their child; they want a clear definition of what their child has. Unfortunately, this can be hard to come by.

Clinicians tend to emphasize *diagnosis* over *definition*. Along with the many open questions about autism, the condition has no concise, widely accepted definition. A diagnosis, on the other hand, focuses on specific clinical criteria. It gives medical experts a label for a condition or disease as identified by its signs, symptoms, and results of various diagnostic procedures. You may have to settle for a diagnosis, but as later chapters explain, over time you will arrive at your own definition of your child's condition.

How Autism Is Diagnosed

The diagnostic criteria for autism are outlined in the *Diagnostic and Statistical Manual of Mental Disorders* (the *DSM*), currently in its revised fourth edition (APA 2000). The *DSM* treats autism as a spectrum disorder, meaning that different individuals with autism are affected differently. Dividing lines between different parts of the spectrum may be blurry. Nevertheless, the *DSM* criteria are broadly consistent with what we mentioned earlier:

people with autism typically have difficulties in verbal and nonverbal communication, impaired social skills, and unusual interests and behaviors.

The *DSM* is periodically refined in a painstaking, multiyear consultative process. Whether it's the fourth or fifth edition when you read this, the most recent version of the *DSM* reflects the prevailing consensus on the definition of autism. Almost any professional making a diagnosis will have been trained using the *DSM*.

Practical Note:
Why You Need to Know about the DSM

In the United States, *DSM* criteria serve as a common reference point for clinicians and researchers. Psychiatrists and other physicians, psychologists, social workers, occupational and rehabilitation therapists, and counselors use it to diagnose patients and select treatments (for more on the diagnostic process, see chapter 5). School administrators may use the *DSM* to allocate educational services; insurance companies use it to define the services they will cover. You do not need to master its details, but once you know that the *DSM* is used in decision making, you can draw on its language to make a case for your child's services. Discuss the terms with your diagnostician and take careful notes. To the extent that it's feasible, check that your diagnostician's written reports match your understanding of your child and invoke the appropriate terminology from the *DSM*.

Despite its use in the field, the *DSM* cannot convey the impact of a condition like autism on the lives of children and their families. For that, we turn to the real experts.

How Should We Describe Autism?

What do people with autism—and those closest to them—consider most important to know about the condition? Many feel that generalizations fail to recognize the specifics of the disorder. You know one person with autism, the saying goes, and you know one person with autism.

Author, artist, and autism consultant Donna Williams was diagnosed with autism only after many difficult years of misdiagnoses and inappropriate treatment. She became a staunch advocate for recognizing the individuality of each person with autism, pointing out that various coexisting conditions make each person's experience different. According to Williams, other peoples' "projections and theories" only partially account for the actual experiences of an individual with autism (www.donnawilliams.net/about.0.html). Her views are echoed by others in the autism community.

Practical Note:
Advocate for Your Child as an Individual

Professional experts too often overlook the unique understanding and insights of ordinary people who live with autism, despite paying lip service to the notion. Many a parent has heard clinicians or school administrators say, "Of course, *you're* the real expert!" only to feel railroaded by the professionals when it comes to making decisions about their child. Learn to present your child's specific profile, both needs and strengths, effectively. Encourage others to see her as more than a diagnosis. Some families prepare a short video, shot on a mobile phone, to show on a laptop at the beginning of a major meeting about their child's treatment and education. A slide show of photos could accomplish the same goal. You'll find a more detailed guide for doing this in writing in chapter 10.

Pairing Useful Insights from Others with a Quest for Specifics

Some would say that the specificity of lived experience and variation in the impact of autism call into question how much you can learn from someone else. And within the autism community, skepticism about generalizations may give rise to cynicism about research conclusions.

On the other hand, to educate others, build awareness, and generate dialogue, it's important to explain autism to others. Ellen Notbohm (2005) drew on her experience as the mother of a boy with autism to write *Ten Things Every Child with Autism Wishes You Knew*. The book struck a chord with many parents and offers a useful starting point for building your own and others' understanding of how your child may experience the world.

Recognizing that any personal understanding of autism is seen through the lens of individual experience, we'll link themes from our clinical overview of autism with a sampling of views from the real world.

The Impact of Autism on a Life: Learning from Others' Experience

We talked to dozens of families and read numerous reports, reflections, and accounts by people with autism and their families to develop a picture grounded in the lived experience of autism.

One person's or one family's subjective experience is, of course, unique, but that doesn't make it less valid than, say, a research study. Yet it can be very difficult to make sense of various one-off accounts, no matter how authentic. Although we've taken a shot at it with the synthesis presented here, we urge you to learn more. For dozens of thoughtful reflections on personal experiences, look at *Voices from the Spectrum: Parents, Grandparents, Siblings, People with Autism, and Professionals Share Their Wisdom*, a collection of essays by people with autism, their parents, grandparents, siblings, and others, edited by Cindy Ariel and Robert Naseef (Jessica Kingsley Publishers, 2006). Another collection, titled *Gravity Pulls You In: Perspectives on Parenting Children on the Autism Spectrum*, includes essays and poems, some of which are beautifully lyrical, edited by Kyra Anderson and Vicki Forman (Woodbine House, 2010).

Another problem in drawing on subjective experience is that we tend to treat views that differ from ours as less valid. Voices from the autism community may not be accorded legitimacy because they do not fit the mold or don't square with formal definitions; some take a strident tone (but, as we discuss at the end of this book, there's much to learn from the community about accepting autism). Interestingly, new technology has allowed many more views to be shared in blogs, online videos, and art presented on the web. For example, vivid and varied real-life accounts featuring ordinary people who have grown up with autism are featured on the UK National Autistic Society website (see recommended reading).

We'll look at five aspects of autism highlighted by people who live with it.

Sensory Issues

What is it like to experience the world with autism? Personal accounts reframe what are ordinary experiences for typically developing people in terms that may resonate. For example, extreme auditory sensitivity may translate daily life into a series of grating sounds; think of the noise made by fingernails on a chalkboard. Sensory issues are not always unpleasant: some people with autism have an uncommon connection among different senses, known as *synesthesia*, where real input from one sense (such as sound) generates a sensory experience that feels just as real in another sense (for example, vision). Seeing numbers as colors or personalities is another example.

For many people with autism, extreme sensitivity makes it difficult or impossible to attend to more than one input at a time: a person may be able to pay attention to vision, sound, or smell, but not all three at once.

Steven, a fifteen-year-old boy, described what he called "intensified senses." For him, lights were brighter, sounds louder, and touch more intense than what others experience. At home, his family kept the lights low and noise levels down. Entering the outside world was difficult, his parents explained. At a crowded mall or busy restaurant, he would get agitated and then seem to shut down. "My mind goes blank," he said, "and I don't remember what happened." On such days, he needed to go home and take a nap. For him, answering a question when his brain was processing and dealing with sensory overload was nearly impossible.

Sensory processing and regulation are difficult for many people with autism. Any sense may generate overwhelmingly strong experiences, such as an extreme reaction to touch, known as *tactile defensiveness*. In other cases, low sensory responsiveness leads a person to seek more stimulation. Sometimes, people with autism can have difficulty identifying their own internal states—for instance, not knowing whether they're hungry. At its worst, managing sensory effects can take up most of a person's attention and effort, leaving him unable to manage any additional demands (often referred to as "sensory overload").

How do you cope with a world that's so challenging?

Stimming

Think of what you do when things get really difficult. How do you soothe yourself? Exercise is a healthy activity, but in moments of stress, you may turn to nail-biting (or chocolate!). Behaviors that help you manage an overload of sensory inputs or external demands are informally called "stims" in the autism community. The term refers to both self-calming and self-stimulating behaviors and activities that are thought to help people maintain an appropriate level of arousal. People with autism may flap their hands, twirl or rock their bodies, hop or spin, or flick objects repeatedly. Echolalia, the tendency to memorize and repeat words, phrases, or even paragraphs, may also be a self-stimulatory behavior.

Eighteen-year-old Charles explained to occupational therapists that when he got anxious, he calmed himself by stimming. His therapist noted that Charles would clap or flap his hands, rock his body, or spin a ball for hours. Being made to stop made him feel anxious and unleashed an unpleasant sense of pressure, Charles explained. Stimming allowed him to feel his body. He felt alive because his hands were flapping; "Your hands can't flap if you are not alive" is how he put it.

If stimming is what it takes for you to handle the world, imagine the difficulty of controlling it. When they most need to stim, adults and children with autism who are trying to fit in at work or school must restrain themselves. It may be possible to turn a preferred form of self-soothing behavior into something more socially acceptable: fidgeting with a small item in your pocket instead of flicking an object, for instance. But it's not easy to do.

Problem Behaviors

Behaviors that may seem to be bad habits, inexplicable, or even willfully odd may actually be functional for the person with an ASD. Adults on the autism spectrum urge us to treat apparently strange behaviors as attempts to communicate or control what feels to them like chaos or sensory overload.

When sensory and other challenges are too much to manage, one response is social withdrawal: retreating into your own world. Another result may be disruptive, socially unacceptable, or even violent behavior. Of course, plenty of people with autism are never violent, and there are violent people who do not have autism, but there are people with autism who engage in behaviors that harm themselves or others. Some children with ASDs exhibit self-injurious behaviors; for example, a child might bang her own head against a wall or injure her own eyes. Unfortunately, difficulty in communicating can make it hard to identify the triggers. Behavioral strategies can help, as we will see later.

For family members, understanding autism involves trying to appreciate the function of seemingly strange behaviors.

Unusual Interests

Unusually focused and limited activities and interests are, for many, part and parcel of having autism. One child lined up dinosaurs as soon as he returned from school every day; another learned all she could about Civil War clothing. On meeting a friend for lunch, a professional launched into a long speech about a mathematical idea that was really interesting to her but not to her lunch companion.

Intense interests are not necessarily a bad thing: nowadays, entrepreneurs and inventors may credit their success to a narrowness of interests that enables productive concentration. But overly focused interests create challenges. One reason to take them seriously is that they impair social interaction. After the hundredth time your five-year-old talks about Thomas the Tank Engine (from *The Railway Series*), on the playground, other kindergartners may simply steer clear of him. Your child's narrow interests end up restricting his ability to play with, learn from, and enjoy being with his peers.

Challenges in Social Interaction and Communication

Language is inseparable from social interaction, and people with autism typically have problems with language. Yet there may be a real mix of strengths and problems. Your child may be off the charts when it comes to reading words (decoding) but struggle to interpret even the simplest story. Some people with autism are excellent spellers; a few can learn foreign languages easily. Others may have persistent challenges in producing speech or grammatically correct expression, or in understanding spoken and written material. You may notice unusual volume, intonation, and formality in language.

Megan, a sixteen-year-old with Asperger's disorder, became angry and yelled whenever her doctor spoke to her using metaphor or irreverence or gently teased her. Figures of speech confused her. She insisted on concrete instructions and explained that she didn't understand teasing. For her, being called a "silly goose" meant that she was an unintelligent water fowl. Words had very specific meanings to Megan and were often associated with pictures in her head. She was at a loss when it came to making sense of the image triggered by being called a "silly goose."

The social world and language stymie many people with autism, forcing them to play the role of social detective. For instance, Megan could not read her doctor's face when he was being playful. On realizing that she lacked the ability to read faces, she learned instead to listen for variations in voice quality to judge whether someone was mad at her or joking with her.

Deficits in communication and social skills lie at the core of autism. Many people struggle with even the basic tools for developing relationships. This is evident in social interaction: the back-and-forth of a conversation tends to lack fluidly and responsiveness when you are talking to someone with autism. Even for someone who has verbal skills, understanding and using cultural norms, figures of speech and idioms, gestures, eye contact, and body language are real challenges. People with autism are often less capable than their peers of inferring, understanding, and acting on other people's emotions and internal states. Many people with ASDs encounter minefields in the nonverbal and practical aspects of social language.

Megan had a difficult time understanding that if a boy said hello, this did not mean he wanted to date her. It didn't make sense to her that telling people that she had Asperger's wasn't the best way to strike up a conversation. Whenever she met a potential friend, she would immediately start talking about the boys in her school, failing to notice that the other girl did not appear interested. Her experience is emblematic of the vast territory of social interaction that remains uncharted and sometimes seems almost impossibly difficult to navigate for people with autism.

Moving Forward with Understanding and Appreciation

We now have a list of challenges to tackle. In the pages ahead, we'll explain more and offer practical advice. But let's not forget to appreciate what's best in our children. Above all, let's be optimistic. Even children who appear to be severely affected—as Temple Grandin was when she was young—can make incredible progress. In fact, Grandin is living proof that it's possible to take on autism's challenges.

In the end, helping your child may be simpler than you think. Raising a child with autism is not about interventions and treatments. Instead figure out what's most interesting and motivating for your child, and structure what you are doing around that. At the same time, remove or help your child cope with anything that creates anxiety or pain. You'll need to cultivate your curiosity about, aim to understand, and look for practical solutions to the problems that most limit your child's learning and participation.

Like every family, yours is charting its own course. You may discover a diet, program, or protocol that works for your child. To figure out what to try, you'll need hope, empathy, and a few research and detective skills, along with critical thinking and mindfulness. We'll provide practical help with all of these skills in the chapters ahead.

CHAPTER 2

What Causes Autism?

Before we consider treatments, let's look at what causes autism. This chapter presents a short but essential detour designed to help you make sense of the findings and to inform your thinking about treatments and a possible cure.

Almost as soon as they receive a diagnosis, many parents struggle to understand what caused their child's autism. It's natural to seek explanations, but the quest may be quixotic. And the question can distract families from focusing on treatments and interventions.

The media may not help. Dramatic headlines capture the latest assertion about autism, only to become yesterday's news. For instance, a 1998 study by physician Andrew Wakefield and his colleagues found a link between autism and a vaccine given to infants. His findings were published by the prominent medical journal the *Lancet*. The study was small, with only twelve children, yet the ensuing media reports raised such alarm that it put parents off vaccinating their children. At the time, many praised Wakefield's work.

In 2010, in a dramatic reversal, the *Lancet* retracted the earlier study, stating that Wakefield had made false claims about how the study had been conducted. This, again, made media headlines—this time vilifying the physician as a fraud.

How the Evidence Stacks Up

The question of what causes autism bedevils researchers. One consideration is the increasing number of children who are receiving an ASD diagnosis. Any explanation for autism must account for its growing incidence, so some research focuses on population-level studies in epidemiology to identify broad changes. Other studies address mechanisms within an individual's anatomy and physiology that could explain how autism originates.

The Search for an Explanation

The truth is that today there are no clear answers about what causes autism. Scientists look to two broad categories of factors: (a) genetics and (b) everything else, including environmental factors that can have an impact on a child's development even in the womb. It is generally accepted that autism is caused by a combination of both genetic and environmental factors. Some parents find this explanation insufficient and seek certainty concerning what caused autism in their child. In coming to your own assessment of what caused autism in your child, it's important that you understand the strengths and limitations of science.

Scientific research offers our only hope for uncovering the cause. Even if its practice is sometimes imperfect, research that follows scientific methodology can help us assess whether one potential explanation is better than another. As many explanations are tested, our overall understanding improves. Not every study, even if published in a reputable journal, will withstand the test of time. Provisional explanations are sometimes confirmed by follow-up studies, but other times, their limitations are exposed by subsequent research. A theory that has only shaky evidence today may one day find more support in the research that follows. It's important to know what to take seriously. With this in mind, let's dispel some myths.

What Doesn't Cause Autism

Research databases and popular media offer a plethora of claims and counterclaims about the causes of autism. Although we can't possibly discuss everything that doesn't cause this disorder, we'll take a look at some of the more influential or curious claims.

Vaccines and Vaccine Preservatives

In the debate about what is causing the rise in autism, no single factor has been as scrutinized or is as controversial as childhood vaccines. The American Academy of Pediatrics, the Centers for Disease Control and Prevention, and the National Institutes of Health state that there is no relationship between vaccines and autism (Immunization Safety Review Committee 2004). Nevertheless, as recently as 2010, 25 percent of parents still believed that vaccines caused autism (Freed et al. 2010).

Without question, vaccines have saved countless lives and are essential for the well-being and health of society. Even those researchers who suspect a connection to autism do not support skipping vaccines, but argue that they should be made safer. But why and how are vaccines and autism even linked?

Vaccines are designed to resemble disease-causing organisms like viruses and bacteria. If you are not vaccinated, some diseases can cause serious illness or even death if you are exposed to them. Vaccines prepare your immune system against a full invasion by the real virus or bacteria by triggering the formation of antibodies: chemical armies ready to fight potentially dangerous infections. Vaccines include preservatives to prevent their contamination from the growth of microorganisms. Although thirty years ago, vaccine manufacture was less sterile and preservatives were essential, nowadays they are less needed. One preservative used between the late 1980s and 2003 was thimerosal, a mercury-based preservative. Mercury is toxic to the nervous system, and children exposed to it before birth may be born with brain development disorders. The toxin appears to affect development by preventing cells from finding their normal place in the brain. Children who died after exposure to high levels of mercury were found to have lost cells throughout the brain.

Researchers theorized that some children's bodies could not handle even very small amounts of mercury and that multiple vaccinations over the years caused mercury to accumulate in their bodies. The researchers argued that the resulting toxic level of mercury not only disrupted brain development but also harmed intestinal lining. Their theory was that the resulting "leaky gut" could not properly protect the body against other toxins, including chemicals from foods that were otherwise benign.

The CDC responded with additional research, finding that thimerosal alone could not account for the rise in autism (Price et al. 2010). Millions of children had received these vaccines without developing obvious brain problems. Nevertheless, the concern led to the removal of mercury from almost all vaccines. Yet in the years since its removal, rates of autism have continued to rise.

Other External Causes That Are Discredited, Unsupported, Or Still Unknown

We mentioned the discredited "refrigerator mother" theory in chapter 1, noting that parenting is no longer thought to play a role in autism.

In recent years, researchers have looked at overall trends in their search for a cause. For example, autism became more prevalent over the same time period that cell phone usage went up. A statistical study found correspondence in the patterns of growth in cell phone usage and rates of autism (Mariea and Carlo 2007). A correlational study like this one can show similarities in behavior patterns over time but cannot establish cause.

A similar approach was taken by a team of economists who found that rates of autism were increased in areas with higher levels of television watching (Waldman, Nicholson, and Adilov 2006). The fact that both factors had increased is far from evidence that watching TV causes autism. We can debate the quality of what's on TV, but science has not shown that a parent's or child's television watching causes autism.

Is stress a factor? We know that such life events as divorce, family conflict, job loss, pregnancy, and financial problems can cause stress in families. Although many families experience daily stress and we know that stress has an impact on mood and behavior, which affect the brain, none of these specific stressors has been shown to cause autism. To be clear, divorce does not cause autism, a parent's job loss does not cause autism, and so on.

The Continuing Search For External Causes

We'll next consider research on genetic causes of autism. But first, it's worth mentioning that other environmental factors under investigation include prenatal exposure to chemicals, infection, and medications. Some of these factors may be shown to contribute to autism. It's possible that one of the factors discussed previously will come into play somehow. Remember, any potential contributing cause will not, by itself, determine whether someone develops autism, but instead increase the probability that a child would later be diagnosed with autism.

What May Cause Autism

Autism appears to involve an interaction between the environment and genes. In 10 percent or less of all cases, autism is linked to a separate diagnosable medical condition (Hallmayer et al. 2011). In the future this proportion will likely rise as diagnostic capabilities improve. To give you a sense of the current understanding, we provide an overview of a few conditions that are related to autism, including some with known genetic causes, and discuss the emerging genetic research.

Genetics

It's becoming increasingly clear that genetics is important, yet no single gene is responsible for autism. Given the complexity of the brain and the variety and number of genes responsible for its formation, it seems likely that autism involves a number of genes.

From a genetic perspective, if a child has autism, there is an increased risk that another child born to the same parents will also have it (from a base rate of around 0.7 percent, the sibling rate is 4 to 10 percent [ibid.]). In identical twins, if one has autism, the risk of the other having autism is higher (58 percent in a recent study [ibid.]; as high as 95 percent in others [Bertoglio and Hendren 2009]). But this also implicates something other than genes in autism. Because identical twins have exactly the same genetic code, if genes alone caused autism, we would expect every twin of a person with autism to also have the condition. As this is not the case, something else must also be at work.

What gene studies show. Identifying a genetic cause could enable a test to identify children who are at risk. Because today the diagnosis relies on a child's behavior, it can be many years before parents know that the child has autism. A genetic test could allow much earlier intervention for an at-risk child and offer valuable input to parents who must make difficult family choices.

Meanwhile, keeping up with every new finding on genes and autism was nearly impossible during the writing of this book; we regularly came across updated research and new genetic discoveries. Much of the research pinpoints variations in how genes play out in the body. If genes vary, the brain and body develop differently, and the child's capacities and behavior vary as a result.

We'll look at just a sampling of the research. One study (Arking et al. 2008) of thousands of children with autism showed that many had variations of a gene that makes a protein that is essential for brain cells to grow connections. Such connections may be important for cognitive, sensory, and social domains. Another study linked the gene for the production of oxytocin, a chemical that promotes bonding in mammals, to autism (Park et al. 2010). Genes that control speech and language in the brain may be affected in people with autism (Mukamel et al. 2011), along with the genes that make serotonin, a brain chemical associated with depression and behavior (Kistner-Griffin et al. 2011). It would take an entire book to spell out every finding. Instead, we refer you to the Autism Genome Project at autismgenome.org. We suspect that the study of genetics will continue to yield many clues.

One genetic theory: Assortative mating. In 2006, Simon Baron-Cohen, of Cambridge University, proposed a theory that had been discussed informally for years. Acknowledging that it was controversial, he argued that it nevertheless warranted investigation. The idea was based on data: a survey had found that children with autism were twice as likely as their typical peers to have fathers and grandfathers who worked with computers or in engineering. Compared with their classmates who were studying the humanities, students in the natural sciences and mathematics had more relatives with autism. Mathematicians had a higher rate of conditions on the autism spectrum than the general population.

Labeling these domains the "systematizing professions," Baron-Cohen suggested that there was a link between autism and aptitude in engineering, mathematics, computer science, and natural science. The connection could explain the rise in autism as follows: if people in these professions meet each other in their high-tech jobs, get together, and mix their genes, more people like them will be born. People who share common characteristics tend to produce children with similar characteristics. For instance two tall people are likelier to have taller-than-average children. So the assortative mating idea is that the children of two people who tend to systematize will have a double dose of the genes that produced social difficulties in their parents. The idea is certainly interesting, but the evidence is not yet documented.

Maternal and paternal age. Maternal and paternal age is a risk factor for the development of autism (Croen et al. 2007). The older the parent, the higher the risk. Some researchers think that genes alter with age, whereas others think that older people accumulate environmental toxins over time that give rise to genetic differences.

Medical Conditions With Symptoms That Overlap With Autism

Several medical conditions look very similar to autism but differ in important ways. We mention a few here to underscore the implications for parents. To diagnose autism and rule out these other conditions, simply assessing behavior may not be enough. Other tests may be needed. Getting the correct diagnosis is important because treatment options and decisions may depend on it. In some cases, parents will look to other approaches besides those presented in this book.

Landau-Kleffner syndrome (LKS). Also known as acquired epileptic aphasia, LKS is a seizure disorder accompanied by the loss of skills such as speech and the emergence of autistic behaviors. At first there is a gradual or sudden decline in the ability to understand and use spoken language. Kids with LKS have abnormal brain waves that can be detected with an electroencephalogram (EEG), which reads the electric activity of the brain. Because not all people with LKS have seizures and some people with autism have EEG abnormalities, LKS can look like autism.

In some cases of LKS, complete language recovery has been reported from just a few days to a couple of years after onset. Usually, however, language problems continue into adulthood. Most children with LKS outgrow their seizures, with electrical brain activity on the EEG returning to normal by age fifteen. If LKS is misdiagnosed as autism, the person may appear to have made a remarkable recovery.

Fragile X syndrome. Fragile X syndrome is the most common inherited form of mental retardation. The syndrome is caused by a difference in a single gene, which can be passed from one generation to the next. The symptoms occur because the gene cannot produce enough of a protein needed by brain cells to develop and function normally. The clearest impact of the condition is on intelligence. More than 80 percent of males with the syndrome have an IQ of 75 or less (Hagerman and Hagerman 2002). In females, however, the effect of fragile X on intelligence is more variable, and some girls with fragile X have normal IQs.

Most children with fragile X have social anxiety, resulting in extreme nervousness, avoidance of eye contact, and disorganized speech. People with fragile X try to avoid social situations. It will often take them longer to get back to their nonanxious state than typical, unaffected children. Boys with fragile X are easily upset and overwhelmed by sights and sounds—for instance, in busy urban settings. Changes in routine are difficult to manage for children with fragile X, and some become rigid, tense, or moody in response. When severely agitated, they can have tantrums or exhibit repetitive actions, such as rocking back and forth and biting themselves, behaviors that are often found in children with autism. Girls' symptoms tend to be milder and less pronounced. It's easy to see how autism might be misdiagnosed as fragile X. Unlike autism, fragile X syndrome can be diagnosed using a blood test for the gene known as FMR1.

Tuberous sclerosis complex (TSC). This is a rare genetic disease that causes tumors to grow in the brain and other organs. According to the National Institute of Neurological Disorders and Stroke (NINDS) (2011), up to two-thirds of people with TSC have learning disabilities. When the condition involves the brain, affected children can have low IQ scores. Between 25 and 61 percent of people with TSC also meet criteria for autism, and an even higher percentage are broadly diagnosed with an ASD (Harrison and Bolton 1997). Unfortunately there are no genetic tests or blood tests for the condition. The diagnosis is made clinically on the basis of finding tumors in various parts of the body.

Other medical conditions. Rett's disorder, closed head injuries, brain tumors, brain infections, brain toxins, and other conditions have to be considered too. It's important to share as much information as possible with clinicians to establish a comprehensive history so that all potential causes can be examined, including genetic conditions. Genetic counseling can help not only during the diagnosis of your child but also when you are considering having more children.

Other Medical Factors That May Play A Role

We've considered how genetics and certain medical conditions may be related to autism. As studies in those areas continue, another frontier of research explores potential roles of different parts of the body and of the environment.

The immune system. Antibodies are proteins formed by the body to fight off infections. Sometimes antibodies mistakenly fight against a person's own body, resulting in an autoimmune disorder, such as rheumatoid arthritis or lupus. Immunologists from the MIND Institute at the University of California, Davis, found that immune system problems, including immune reactions in the brain, are associated with autism in a significant subset of children (Ashwood, Wills, and van de Water 2006). It is still not known how or whether the immune system plays a role in the development of autism.

The gastrointestinal (GI) system. Although in the past, it was thought that up to 25 percent of children with autism had GI problems, more recent and rigorous studies, such as one by researchers at the Mayo Clinic (Ibrahim et al. 2009), find no increase in GI symptoms over typically developing children. They discovered that two specific problems were more common in children with autism: constipation and feeding issues. Self-limited diets lacking in fiber and water intake explained the GI symptoms. Nevertheless, because the gut and the brain share important aspects of biology and neurochemicals, research into the GI tract continues, although there's still little evidence of any causal role.

Prenatal stress. Earlier we stated that potential stressors like divorce, job loss, and family arguments do not cause autism. What about the effects of stress itself? Research suggests that prenatal exposure to stress may increase the chance that autism will develop later. Animal studies (Weinstock 2002) show that prenatal stress can produce behaviors that resemble the symptoms of autism. Prenatal stress can also lead to learning and immune-system problems, which are found at higher rates in people with autism. Further, prenatal stress appears to reduce the number of nerve connections in the developing brain, particularly in those areas of the brain that are less active in people with autism. Neither the extent to which nor the mechanism by which prenatal stress might give rise to autism is known. However, because prenatal stress can affect brain development, finding ways to reduce stress benefits an expecting mother and her unborn child.

Looking into the Future

We mentioned interacting effects, suggesting that genetics and environment likely work in tandem to cause autism. If a child is genetically vulnerable, it's possible that encountering one or more other factors—medical problems, stress, immune-system problems, toxins, infective agents, or some as yet unidentified agent—at a specific point in brain development would trigger a cascade of events that leads to autism. Realistically, it will be years before we know whether this theory is correct. It's impossible to completely protect children and parents from exposure to every risk factor in the world, but we know that as science narrows in on the causes, we will be able to better protect children in the future.

With so many concerns, what is a parent to do? The important thing to remember is that autism is a complex condition. Don't be led astray by a headline trumpeting a single cause. If you find an interesting article, discuss it with your health care team. If you are concerned about vaccines, ask your child's doctor about delaying vaccinations or spreading them out. If you are concerned about genes, speaking to a genetic counselor might be useful. Approach the risk factors with common sense and make the most of your team to choose what to investigate. And develop your own perspective of your goals for your child: if not a cure, what are you seeking?

CHAPTER 3

Can Autism Be Cured?

Type the word "autism" into an online search engine, and the advertisements pop up. "I conquered autism," reads one; "Autism can be cured," reads another. Turn on the TV, and there's a news story you might have seen before. It's about a boy who had been completely noncommunicative and "severely autistic" at the age of two. The camera turns to a happy six-year-old playing with friends, doing his homework, and having a fun, interactive discussion with his family as he eats a totally normal dinner, spinach included. "You'd never know," marvels the reporter, "that this is the same child." The segment closes with the parents noting that "he no longer has a diagnosis."

The boy was cured, it seems, and what you see on the web reinforces the point: you are supposed to be able to cure your child.

It turns out that the evidence disagrees. Curing autism is no simple matter. Most children who are diagnosed with autism will continue to experience the challenges that place them on the spectrum. Despite superhuman efforts by parents, few children can be completely rescued from the diagnosis.

Understanding why a cure is elusive may help as you consider your next steps and the journey ahead. You'll develop your own perspective on the questions surrounding cures, treatments, and therapies, and what these mean for your family. Life can improve greatly for children who are diagnosed with autism, even if they are never fully "cured."

What Do We Mean by "Cure"?

First, there's a matter of terminology. What do we mean by "cure"? Do autism therapies cure? What would a child who is cured of autism look like?

Traditionally, the term refers to ending a medical condition. If someone has appendicitis, with the right treatment, appendicitis can be cured. If you're cured of something, not only do you no longer have the symptoms, but also the underlying physical causes of the condition have changed permanently. This is not to say that there's no trace—the missing appendix is a clue that you've had appendicitis—but the prime cause of the disease is gone.

Cure and Cause Are Linked

To tackle questions about curing autism, we need to consider what is known about its cause. For most curable medical conditions, the underlying problem is known. If autism had a single physical cause—heavy metal poisoning, leaky gut, a single gene—a cure would be feasible. We'd consider chelation (chapter 9), treatments involving the GI tract (chapter 9), or gene therapy. But as we've just seen, there is no evidence yet that the cause of autism can be reduced to a single factor. The best current thinking is that autism is caused by complex, interacting effects that involve the brain. The disorder is unlikely to have a simple, single cure.

Good News, Bad News: The Brain Is a Special Case

The involvement of the brain in autism is another reason a cure is elusive. Modern research techniques are revealing more about how the brain works, changes, and responds to treatment, but in many ways the brain is still a puzzle. Promising studies show that injured brains can make remarkable recoveries. This ability of the brain to adapt is called *neuroplasticity*. Medical treatments can shape the brain, but what we do also matters.

People's behavior and habits can affect the progression of Alzheimer's disease, for example.

As we saw in the previous chapter, the brains of people with autism appear to develop differently. Is there a chance to correct the course? Because most newly diagnosed people are young and their brains are still developing, there is great interest in treatments that could actually change the brain. The belief that young brains change more readily than older ones creates a sense of urgency for some parents. They feel incredible pressure to act during the period of maximum neuroplasticity. Fortunately the evidence suggests that brains are more malleable throughout the life cycle than previously thought. You have time.

To deliver an actual cure, autism treatments would need to permanently alter brain structure and change many interactions within the brain and its functions. At present we see limited evidence that autism treatments change the brain discernibly. If we don't even know how the brain is involved in autism, how can we sort out what treatments would change the brain?

There's another broad point to keep in mind. When it comes to brain disorders, psychiatrists agree that most people cannot be fully cured. Consider depression. There is evidence that in some cases, antidepressants *may* cure first-time depression such that the person never gets depressed again, but it's much more common for depression to recur or persist. This is not to say that things are hopeless: in many cases, mental illness and brain disorders can be managed, symptoms can be alleviated, and new habits and behavioral changes can generate ongoing improvement, making life easier to navigate.

Can Noncurative Interventions Permanently Improve the Condition?

An intervention that enables learning, adaptation, and development can make life more manageable, even if it falls short of a cure. This is true to some extent in all chronic diseases. In diabetes, diet and exercise can improve the body's ability to manage blood sugar levels. Along with a reduction in weight and blood pressure, these steps can change the severity of a person's diabetes diagnosis and overall prognosis.

In autism, there's another twist to the story. Compensatory treatments may improve the underlying condition. For instance, teaching someone with no spoken language skills some sign language may improve his ability to communicate, so sign language appears to be an adaptive aid. But teaching sign language may also affect brain development in such a way as to eventually enable speech. So the intervention goes beyond supporting the current state of functioning to deliver something therapeutic.

With continued use, adaptive aids may end up helping shift the brain a little. In these circumstances, such interventions function as both support and cure. This is one reason treatment, intervention, and cure are so complex for conditions like autism. Educational and social-communication interventions may not seem like medical cures at all, yet they are thought to affect the brain over time, leading to gradual improvement. But the processes are still not well understood, and nothing's guaranteed.

How about Cures That Affect the Brain Indirectly?

Parents have been paying attention to potential autism cures that affect the body as a whole. Consider dietary changes or chemical interventions such as chelation. Their proponents argue that they change the brain via indirect mechanisms.

Here's a word on why mechanisms matter. We use the term to refer to the sequence of specific changes in the body that are brought about by an intervention. We look at mechanisms to explain the specifics of how a given intervention affects a person's body and brain, and from there, her learning and behavior. The sequence of steps for how this plays out tells you a story; that's what we mean by "mechanism." Unfortunately many mechanisms are simply impossible to observe directly. We're left instead with having to guess at them, hypothesize what the intermediate and final effects might be, and then look for clues that these effects are happening.

Treatments that affect different parts of the body, if they are to cure autism, would have to affect the brain in a systematic and permanent way. For most treatments—new or old—these mechanisms are simply not known.

Will We Stumble upon a Cure?

It's possible that someone, someday, will, by sheer random luck, discover a cure for autism. In theory, you could find a cure without knowing the cause and without being able to verify mechanisms. In all cases, to be confident that what we're looking at is indeed a cure, we have to hold science and medicine to high standards of evidence, such as those discussed in chapter 8.

The burden of proof is even higher when neither cause nor mechanism is clear. There's no question that in the past, doctors, parents, researchers, and others collectively failed to build strong enough evidence for proposed causes and cures. In one era, mothers were blamed for their children's autism. In another era, the belief that vaccines cause autism was not sufficiently challenged. In both cases, the courses of treatment suggested by each belief failed to bring children back to normalcy, and families suffered as a result.

The medical and scientific professions deserve some of the blame, but tightening their research standards cannot be the entire solution. Parents have an important role to play as recipients of expert advice and advocates for their children. In chapter 7 we provide a list of questions to ask anyone who recommends a treatment or "cure." You can not only help ensure that your child gets the best treatment, but also help hold the field to the highest standards. You are an important part of the system!

What's the Evidence for Any Form of Long-Term Improvement?

To help you develop a commonsense approach grounded in evidence, we'll survey interventions and treatments for which research shows beneficial long-term impact. We'll also offer some advice on what to do when the evidence is unclear.

The research varies widely. Almost 40 percent of parents responding to a large-sample survey said that a family member at one point diagnosed with an ASD no longer had the condition (Kogan et al. 2009). This study is self-reported, meaning that there was no check on what parents told the surveyors. In more fine-grained studies of people over time, the evidence differs. In 2009 Daniel Geschwind showed that over 70 percent of children diagnosed with autism failed to reach independent status. Can both results be true? Because the studies were so different, the answer is not known.

What interventions make a difference? There are parents and practitioners who claim that children who were diagnosed appropriately with an ASD have been cured of autism with alternative treatments such as diets, supplements, or chelation. Most of the evidence about long-term improvement supports interventions that address learning and interaction. When given a program of applied behavior analysis (ABA) interventions, children build skills, and small studies suggest that many acquire enough skills to succeed in regular-education classrooms (Sallows and Graupner 2005; Dawson et al. 2010).

Why It's So Difficult to Know for Sure

Progress in medicine often starts with an idea about the underlying mechanism causing the disease or condition. If initial explorations of the ideas are promising, the next step is to develop treatments that are tested to see if they work better than the alternatives. But research on ASD treatment is stymied from the start by our current lack of knowledge about autism's causes.

Another barrier to research is finding a large enough number of patients and families to participate. In chapter 8, you'll learn more about double-blind, placebo-controlled studies; these can take years. And there are practical and ethical barriers. Can you really tell one family not to be concerned about mercury intake, while telling another to completely avoid exposure to mercury? Vaccinating some kids and not others in a study would place unvaccinated children at unacceptable risk of measles or hepatitis B.

Finding Your Path When Studies Fall Short

How do you make sense of the patchwork of studies, some of which yield contradictory advice? It can be perplexing to follow the news, which, these days, seems to take a blow-by-blow approach to presenting research. Headlines highlight debates and controversies instead of emerging consensus. What if today's big news turns out to be wrong, perhaps even damaging, tomorrow?

It's easy to imagine a conspiracy at work when the statistics and science are so confusing, particularly when the government and drug companies are involved. Ultimately, approaches that work will stand the test of time, and those that are no good will not. Cultivate a bit of skepticism regarding the latest headline about cause or cure, but steer clear of paranoia. It's a fine line to follow!

Practical Note:
Making Sense of New Information about Cause and Cure

Here are some strategies for navigating this area.

Be skeptical of one-off studies. If you look at the research yourself, try to find evidence that seems to be accumulating, rather than look at the controversies highlighted in news stories. Several panels of experts have done such analyses in recent years: look for consensus reports and meta-analyses. Also consider the sample size. A study of three or twelve children is unlikely to provide sufficient evidence.

Draw on your team. You don't have to be the expert; you just need to ask the questions. Your child's doctor or other specialist is trained to identify the key findings and screen out what is not yet time tested. This is part of the training for clinicians and professional therapists; use their expertise!

Tap into the wisdom of a group. Interacting with others is a great strategy. Can you stay up to date with current findings and explore your thinking by participating in a support group? Online discussions or parent groups could help you sort out your assessment by discussing your interpretations with others. A group forum can enable parents to argue various perspectives and explore alternatives.

Learn how to make sense of statistics. As a parent, you also need to figure out what works for your child. If 60 percent of people improved with a certain treatment, then 40 percent did not; chances are pretty good that your child won't. On the other hand, your child might be the one who responds to a particular treatment, even if others don't.

Be skeptical of any great anecdote, no matter how vivid. Devotion to one approach may make sense if it works for your child and you have the supporting evidence. Signing up for an approach just because someone tells a great story or is personally compelling does not make sense.

We want to help you develop a view of autism that is useful to *you*. Your own understanding of your child is crucially important—as is your understanding of the current knowledge of the condition. While science and medicine still wrestle with open questions, the people most directly affected by autism, including their families, are on the front lines of exploring new treatments and interventions. This practical experience may turn out to be critical in the quest for a cure, and researchers are finding new ways to tap into this experience by collaborating with affected individuals and families.

Here's our final word of advice on this subject: don't let your quest for a cure distract you from the many possibilities for improvement promised by the interventions that have been developed over recent decades. Even if a full-on cure isn't in the cards, you can help your child live a better life.

If Not a Cure, Then What Are We Aiming For?

If you accept that a simple cure will be elusive, what are you left with? Are parents supposed to give up? Or are there other goals to consider? Along with symptomatic relief, parents seek a measure of improvement that they may call "recovery" or "losing the diagnosis." Other families set their sights on increasing independence, and many mention happiness and fulfillment. We'll take a practical look at the broad goals set by families of children with autism—goals that may fall short of a complete cure but represent realistic and practical aspirations.

Practical Note:
Four Types of Aspirations for the Family of a Child with Autism

Symptomatic relief. Should we settle for simply reducing symptoms? Parents of children on the spectrum do not take this question lightly. Symptomatic relief is important. For many, reducing the most painful effects of autism brings about real improvements for both child and family.

Losing the diagnosis. If, after treatment, your child no longer meets the criteria for an autism diagnosis, you may consider this to be a recovery. Some parents tell us that they would like their child to be able to "pass" in the everyday world. Every type of treatment has its own advocates. We'll consider behavioral approaches as an example.

Applied behavior analysis (ABA) does not rest on a mechanism-based view; there's no complex underlying psychological model. The approach seeks to train children to respond appropriately to the world around them. ABA trains children to take specific actions in given settings and situations, from academic to social. By teaching kids explicitly what to do, ABA programs have been shown to deliver real results. The most successful children in intensive ABA programs lose their diagnoses over the course of several years (Howard et al. 2005). It's one intervention with a body of published evidence in its favor (NAC 2011).

However, if your son loses his diagnosis, will he look like a typically developing child? Chances are he'll always be different. That's not necessarily a bad thing! What if a paper-and-pencil test shows that your son continues to meet autism criteria, but thanks to intensive intervention, he gets by in the world just fine? Is he still autistic?

Avoid all-or-nothing thinking in this area. Diagnostic criteria for conditions as complex as autism are limited in their ability to represent the whole child. Your child is not a diagnosis.

While we encourage every family to intensively implement the interventions they think will most likely help their child overcome the diagnosis, it's wise to treat the notion of full recovery with some skepticism. Perhaps some children who have lost the diagnosis were initially misdiagnosed.

Perhaps the child was trained to pass diagnostic tests but still falls short of typical behavior in the real world. Gains in one area may not be matched in others. A bright child may be able to handle schoolwork but have "odd" behaviors and emotional outbursts that lead to social difficulties with peers.

A child's functioning relative to his peers may look different over time. When he is young, he may fit in with his fellow preschoolers, but his differences may be more evident alongside neurotypical classmates in later grades. By the time he's in college, he may find a more comfortable place where he fits in.

Another reason to remain somewhat skeptical of recovery is that developmental and other changes can have profound impact. A preschool child who has lost his diagnosis by the time he gets to kindergarten may encounter new challenges at puberty, when shifting hormones change the body and brain. Set your sights on recovery, but treat the notion with caution.

Functioning, participation, and independence. Instead of searching for a cure, or even recovery, many families choose to focus on their children's ability to more effectively function in their environments. This may be a more attainable and practical goal. For a grade-schooler, the goal may be to participate in regular-education classrooms. For a teenager, learning how to take the bus or to order a meal at a fast-food restaurant may be the goal. For many parents of children with autism, it's their child's life at age twenty-two and beyond that concerns them, once they are no longer under the care of the school system. What will they do all day? Where will they live? Will they be able to earn an income?

Rather than worry about the future, equip yourself by learning about the options, talking to parents of older children, and tapping into the professionals and experts in your area. But at the same time, set practical and realistic medium-term goals, and work toward them. Focusing on practical progress is one of the most effective things you can do for your child and yourself, because it helps align the family, set criteria for decisions, and evaluate improvement.

Happiness and fulfillment. Parents hope that their children will be happy and have good lives. We tend to assess our own success in terms of our children's achievements. Parents of typically developing kids may focus on their academic, athletic, or musical performance. Parents of children with autism choose their own milestones. We run the danger of missing other opportunities if we pay attention only to the specific, narrowly defined achievements we've focused on without considering other paths to happiness and fulfillment.

Yet, there's something to be said for setting goals. As parents, we shape our children. We push them to do things they don't want to do. Our goals as parents come from our own ways of thinking about what it means to be a successful person. These beliefs tell us what to push for, because it's our job to get our kids to do the things that we think are important even when they do not agree: flossing, homework, eating vegetables, writing thank-you notes.

For parents of children with autism, the question of what to push for is rarely simple. What if your preteen appears perfectly happy on his own, playing the same Sesame Street video game hour after hour? Is it right to push him to do something that makes him less happy?

Every family comes up with their own ideas of what matters. Even within the same family, parents push for different things. Cultivating a habit of mindfulness, as we'll discuss next, is one way to help ensure that you are pushing for the right things. Mindfulness can allow you to recognize well-worn patterns of thinking. Habitual behaviors and thoughts are taken for granted, because they are passed down from your family experience and society at large. Part of your new challenge is to sort out what to keep and what to set aside.

CHAPTER 4

Difficulty, Stress, and Our Advice for You

No one can predict what parenting will be like. Think of a first-time parent: you, some years ago. What did you picture as you imagined raising your child? Did you have a sense of the decisions and challenges, not to mention the bills, to come? Did you anticipate what would bring you joy as a parent? Few expectant parents have an inkling of everything that's in store for them. Maybe Mother Nature sets things up this way: in pregnancy and early parenthood, the immediate needs of your infant children are most on your mind. These concerns are very different from those of parents of teenagers or first graders. If we knew of everything in advance, we likely couldn't cope!

If parenting involves improvising, what's helpful? Parents tell us they learn by reflecting on their own journeys; from books, experts, and the media; and by interacting with their families (including their own children), religious leaders, teachers, and others.

When it comes to raising a child with autism, the steps in the journey are more uncharted, the advice more confusing, and the challenges greater. Parents of children with autism manage uncertainties and strains beyond those that others encounter. Some simple steps may help you avoid getting stuck, suffering stress, or making poor choices when it comes to handling the emotional, social, financial, and daily life challenges of raising a child with autism.

In dealing with the initial diagnosis and its aftermath, parents work on coming to terms with a new understanding of their family's life. Some experts have suggested that the stages of grief offer a useful guide to how the process may unfold. While not all parents go through such a process, surely all parents of special-needs children, at some point, grapple with a feeling of loss. We don't dwell here on every stress, sorrow, and challenge you may encounter but, instead, assemble some practical suggestions designed to be useful to you throughout your parenting journey. To set the stage for the advice that is the mainstay of this chapter, we begin with an overview of the effects of autism on the family. If you're feeling stress, depletion, or strain, you will feel less alone. We also share a key insight: after an initial period, families often report that things get better. To help you get there, we offer a set of practices designed to address tension and trade-offs and to help you manage your thinking. This practical advice forms the foundation for what follows: our practical tools for making treatment choices and working with others.

An ASD Diagnosis Affects Parents

Parenting a child with autism is harder than parenting a neurotypical child. If you feel a twinge of resentfulness when fellow parents complain about their typically developing kids, you have grounds for thinking that things really *are* different for you. Knowing that you're not alone in feeling stress may help you manage it. The most widely reported effects on parents are strains on resources and stress. We'll take a brief look at each.

Strains on Resources

Laura Schieve and her colleagues (2007) found that parents of children with autism have more problems than parents of other special-needs children in getting the health care, interventions, and therapies their kids need. These challenges and related financial, employment, and time burdens were significantly greater for ASD families, even when compared to families of children with other health needs. An online survey concurred:

80 percent of the 4,295 families polled by the Interactive Autism Network (IAN) (2009) reported that their financial situation was negatively affected by raising a child with autism. Parents reported average annual out-of-pocket treatment costs ranging from around four thousand to over six thousand dollars, depending on the diagnosis. Many also noted negative career effects from taking time off work, giving up a paid job, or interrupting their education. In chapter 1 we saw the tremendous lifetime cost of having autism. It's easy to imagine the result of such strains on resources: stress and depletion.

Stress and the Parent of a Child with an ASD

You are not alone in feeling stressed. Mothers of children with autism experience more stress than mothers of children with fragile X or Down syndrome (Abbeduto et al. 2004). On discovering a similar finding, Annette Estes and her colleagues pinpointed some reasons in a 2009 study: irritability, agitation, crying, inappropriate speech, inability to follow rules, and other behavioral difficulties, rather than the need for help with daily life, were mothers' biggest sources of stress.

What about family stress? Worry about the future topped the list of concerns for nine of every ten parents, according to a 2009 IAN survey. Most parents felt negative impacts from three additional areas: child behaviors, setbacks, and difficulty in getting treatments. Exhaustion and disappointing treatments struck almost half of the parents as negative stressors.

There are practical aspects too. If your child has autism, you likely spend extra time on daily living tasks, working harder than other parents. Yet parents report that this burden doesn't cause the stress that behavioral challenges do.

While much of the research focuses on mothers, fathers of children with ASDs experience stress too, although seemingly at lower levels than mothers. In general, parents of children with autism report greater psychological problems than other parents, and many describe feelings of isolation. Other common challenges include depression, anxiety, and anger.

Physical Health Effects

A Swedish study looked at effects on the health of parents caring for a child with an ASD, finding significant health impact on mothers, especially if the children were hyperactive or had behavior problems (Allik, Larsson, and Smedje 2006). Interestingly, fathers did not experience such health effects. Another research team asked 299 parents to assess their lives in detail. Compared to other parents, parents of children with autism engaged in less physical activity and had worse physical health, along with poorer psychological health and social relationships and lower overall quality of life (Mugno et al. 2007). Parents of children with ASDs experienced significantly more negative health effects than other parents, including those of children with mental retardation or cerebral palsy.

Marriage

If mothers and fathers experience different levels of stress, and if families experience financial, social, psychological, and practical challenges due to autism, it's easy to imagine that autism would affect couples' relationships. Many parents who struggle to cope with a child with an ASD say that there is a cost of stress on the marriage, and some such parents report lower satisfaction with their relationships. Common marital issues include the division of labor and one partner's denial of the diagnosis (IAN 2009).

Findings on divorce are mixed, but the picture is not as bad as you might fear. One study showed that parents of children with ASDs had a higher divorce rate (23 versus 14 percent over a six-year time span). For parents in typical families, the divorce risk falls after the children reach around eight years of age, but for the participating ASD families, there was no drop in divorce rates (Hartley et al. 2010). On the other hand, a much larger survey found no difference in the divorce rate for ASD families. In this study, 36 percent of children with ASDs did not have two married biological or adoptive parents, compared with 35 percent of non-ASD kids (Freedman et al. 2010). Differences in research design may account for the varied findings. Both studies underscore, however, that not only is divorce not inevitable, but also it's not even the norm. In couples who split after an ASD diagnosis, autism was often identified as a contributing factor but rarely the sole cause (Grosso 2011).

Coming Out on the Other Side

You may feel alarmed by what you have just learned, but parenting a child with a chronic disability is not always a negative experience. This is because sometimes parents' difficult experiences allow them to develop new perspectives and attitudes toward the condition.

One study of 175 parents (Bayat 2007) found that most felt that they had become closer to one another and had developed new abilities as a result of having a child with autism. This resilience was hard earned, usually arising only after a period of marked stress following the initial diagnosis. On average, it took about two years after the autism diagnosis to reach this stage of adjustment. It takes time for families to find their new footing.

As parents we learn from our own experience. Mothers of older kids on the spectrum feel better about their quality of life and have less stress than mothers of younger ones (Bebko, Konstantareas, and Springer 1987). Interestingly, fathers don't show this trend. If parents learn to adapt, they handle parenting better. To cope, parents use venting (a form of emotion-based coping), which can be adaptive; but problem-based coping, such as removing a stressor, seems to be even more effective (Pottie and Ingram 2008). This underscores the value of taking a practical, action-oriented approach to tackling problems as they arise.

Drawing on social support enables parents to navigate challenges. Clearly, this is yet another reason to maintain family relationships and friendships. But it may also help just to know that your own challenges will ebb and flow. Along these lines, what experts refer to as "trajectories of well-being" for mothers of children with ASDs vary with the specifics of each child's development and needs as they play out over time. So, if things are difficult one month, they may get better the next; it's not always going to be tough.

Tackling Common Challenges

You already know that a slew of practical and personal challenges confronts parents of kids with autism. But while they may discuss their children's care and treatment needs, many parents we've met tend to downplay their own challenges in managing their lives, their parenting roles, and difficult times. First, you need to handle the tension and stress that accompany the diagnosis and its aftermath. Perhaps more subtle, but likely even more important, is how you choose to approach parenting in the face of autism. Parents wrestle with how to think about and make sense of the challenges in their lives: the trade-offs, the choices, and the ongoing flow of events, disappointments, and opportunities. What's helpful for this journey? Of course, pretty much every family would welcome more money, more time, or both! And experts agree on the widespread need for more financial and practical support for parents of children with autism. Yet some of the most effective antidotes to your parenting challenges may lie in your own hands. We share some simple, field-tested approaches you can start using today to tackle these challenges.

Managing Tension

Stress can creep up on you and begin to feel like a way of life. It's important to pay attention so that you don't slide into a state of ongoing tension. Symptoms of stress include changes in heart rate, blood pressure, and appetite, along with fatigue, headaches, irritability, memory problems, teeth grinding, reduced sex drive, insomnia, stomach problems, social withdrawal, anxiety, and, at its extreme, depression. In the most severe cases, where anxiety and depression are involved, medication and therapy or counseling can help. However, some relatively simple life changes or some new habits are powerful antidotes. These habits not only are effective in lowering stress, but also generate other health benefits and are far less expensive than medication or psychotherapy; in fact, some are free!

Embedding some of the following changes into your life can cut your stress and tension. The following are our favorites. Choose a few to start; then revisit this list occasionally to find some others to try.

Practical Note:
Proven Antistress Habits

Physical exercise: Exercise not only enhances your sense of well-being and reduces illness and disease, but also releases depression-fighting chemicals like serotonin and endorphins.

Sex: Physical intimacy might be the last thing on your mind during moments of stress, but various studies have established that the benefits of sex are numerous and contribute to stress relief. Sex generates a surge in your body's oxytocin, the bonding chemical that leads to improved closeness with your loved ones.

Yoga: Yoga is a practice that combines some of the elements we mention here—breathing exercises, physical exercise, and meditation—and it's an excellent way to reduce stress.

Progressive muscle relaxation: In progressive muscle relaxation, you tense a group of muscles—say your arm or leg, or your abdominal muscles—as you breathe in, and relax them as you breathe out.

Breathing exercises: In a moment of stress, try this simple step before doing anything else: take a moment to pay attention to your breath. It can change the way you feel right then and slow you down enough to avoid acting impulsively.

You can also change the way you breathe. Try taking longer breaths or holding your breath for a few seconds at a time. Slowing your breathing can help slow down your mind and reduce distraction and stress in the moment. The more you practice breathing exercises, the easier they are to do.

Managing Your Thinking

Perhaps the most powerful tool at your disposal is your ability to manage and change your thinking. How you think about things affects how you feel about your experiences; it's also true that how you feel about something affects how you think about it. Part of being human is that we fall into ineffective thinking habits that affect our own happiness and resilience. Although these habits can shape our lives, like most habits they are often not apparent to us.

For example, if your mental response to having a child with autism is to have the same repetitive and negative thoughts about yourself and your child, these thoughts could lead to ongoing fear, anger, or resentment. Repeat them enough, and these negative thoughts can get stuck in your head and affect your overall outlook. Worse is that such thinking can become a self-fulfilling prophecy; so, for instance, a negative thought pattern about your child can lead to the very negative emotions you are trying to avoid.

Our advice to manage your thinking is not intended to downplay the real challenges and difficulties you face, but to remind you that you have a choice about how you think. Once you realize that the choice is yours and that thoughts are not automatic, you'll have another set of tools to draw on. These ideas entered mainstream psychology in recent years and have been shown to reduce tension, spark curiosity, increase compassion, and build your understanding of others' perspectives.

Your child may have challenges that you do not feel ready to accept. Dealing with these challenges and a multitude of others may require you to acknowledge the facts of the matter. For instance, there's no escaping the reality that your resources are finite. A dollar spent on one thing means a dollar less for something else. Time spent with one kid means less time with others. Time off work at one point means less vacation time or personal time in the future, or reduced prospects for career advancement. What can you do about these realities?

Practical Note:
Thinking Habits for Facing Reality

Practice acceptance. Acceptance helps you reduce the tendency to get stuck in negative thinking. Life may be unfair, but dwelling on this won't change that reality. Instead of fighting the reality of your life, practice acceptance. This means taking in, as best you can, your situation— including your child's diagnosis—as it is. Remind yourself that nobody can do it all and nobody's perfect. Without acceptance, you can get so caught up in wishful thinking that you waste time, or you end up basing decisions on an imagined reality instead of a clear-eyed view of the current situation.

Embrace realism. Inject realism into your decisions by testing your assumptions and expectations. For instance, you might set a goal to become an expert in applied behavior analysis (ABA) over the summer or to have your child toilet trained before school starts next month. Ask yourself whether your goals are realistic and your overall to-do list is feasible. Are you trying to do too much? The following questions should help.

- *Have I compromised my ability to focus by trying to do more than I can accomplish while maintaining my health and relationships?*

- *Am I getting enough sleep? Exercise?*

- *Am I trying to do things that could be left to others? Am I letting teachers, therapists, and others do what they do best? Am I getting their advice on what things are best for me to do?*

- *As I add items to our to-do list, am I also reminding myself to choose what not to do? Am I dropping something when I add new tasks and activities?*

Use these questions to develop your own "reality checklist." Put the list where you'll see it and check in regularly.

Becoming More Mindful

Facing reality goes beyond cultivating acceptance and injecting realism into your decision making. Mindfulness, once an unconventional concept, has joined the mainstream as scientific research reveals its benefits. You can become more mindful by building specific types of thinking and noticing, as we'll explain.

Mindfulness is the intentional, nonjudgmental focus of attention on the present moment. We are learning that mindfulness can reduce stress and increase happiness. When you experience stress, you can tend to think negatively of yourself and others. When you practice mindfulness regularly, you become kinder to yourself and more compassionate toward others.

Mindfulness helps parents of children with autism. After completing a course on the philosophy and practice of mindfulness, mothers of children with autism felt more satisfied with their parenting (Singh et al. 2006). The mindful parents found that their children's behavior was less aggressive, more compliant, and less self-injurious. The positive findings from this small study and the broader evidence on mindfulness suggest that it makes sense to try out the following practices.

Practical Note:
Mindfulness 101

Meditate. Meditation helps you develop mindfulness. When you spend even a few minutes focusing your attention on something, such as your breath, you are meditating. While you meditate, notice as judgments and different thoughts come into your mind, and then gently return your mind to your object of focus, in this case your breath. You can focus on anything you want: a flower, a bite to eat, whatever you choose. Simply stay focused, and when your mind wanders, bring it back. Doing this for just ten minutes several times a week can reduce stress.

Focus on the here and now. Pay attention to the present moment and all that comes with it. Notice your physical sensations, your surroundings, and your thoughts. If you can focus on what's happening right now, without resorting to judgments, expectations, your to-do list, or worries about the future, you are being mindful!

The more you practice mindfulness, the better you get at it. Set aside a few minutes each day to become aware. As you become more mindful, you cultivate appreciation, attention, and awareness. Participating more fully in every interaction deepens your relationships. Notice the judgments that you have, as they can be destructive and signify a lack of real curiosity.

We've talked about paying attention to your own thoughts, but it's also important to consider other people's thoughts. It's easy to forget that others see the world differently, especially when it comes to things that are emotionally charged. In difficult situations, rather than react, try to get where your child, partner, pediatrician, or teacher is coming from. Does it make sense that given how the other person thinks about things, she would act that way?

Practical Note:
Thinking about How Others Think

Imagine another perspective. In a quiet moment, close your eyes and picture what it would be like to experience the world as your child. Imagine life as your child sees it. Imagine focusing on a single object, spinning it or examining its details. Imagine being your child's size and seeing things at her eye level, or imagine what it's like for her to experience the textures of clothes and foods. Try to let go of your own perspective.

Reset your attributions. Try adopting the perspective that others, like most of us, generally try to do the best they can. Your partner may be cranky if he hasn't slept well or has been having difficulties at work. It might be easier to judge him as cranky rather than as tired and distracted. What if he can't help but be cranky at this moment? Ask yourself how you would behave under similar circumstances, to challenge your own assumptions. It's all too easy to attribute bad intent to others, yet we tend to let ourselves off the hook for poor behavior by putting it in the context of how we felt at that moment. We tend to forget that others, even our loved ones, have feelings that influence how they respond to situations. Remind yourself that others might see the world differently and that their circumstances and emotions affect their capacity to perform in a given moment.

Striving for a Balanced Mind-Set

Every child and every family is different, and there's no set answer concerning what's best to do. Know that you will not always make the right choice. Your timing will sometimes be off. Even if you make the right choices, you may not be able to make sense of the results. For instance, you may end up trying different treatment approaches simultaneously, which makes it tough to distinguish what works from what doesn't. The effects of treatment are not always immediate, so you may have to wait before you can assess whether something is working. The sense of urgency that many parents feel in the aftermath of their child's diagnosis only compounds such challenges. Two more ideas can help you build a mind-set to tap into your own wisdom and cultivate a balanced perspective.

Practical Note:
Building a Balanced Mind-Set

Cultivate curiosity. Researchers Jon Allen, Peter Fonagy, and Anthony Bateman (2008) termed a capacity for understanding how others think "mentalizing." Here's something to try when you're stuck in a difficult interaction with someone else: wonder how the other person's thoughts and feelings might have led her to the particular behavior at issue. Instead of relying on guessing or assumptions about how someone else interprets the world, mentalizing involves inquiring and being curious about others. As you do this, you draw on your ability to think about what goes on in the mind of another. Mentalizing also forces you to recognize how your own mind works. All of this wondering can help you cultivate a habit of curiosity. And when you are less certain about your assumptions, others are more willing to work with you.

Aim for compassion. Try seeing your child as perfect. This exercise strengthens your compassion for her. This practice may be difficult at first. You may try to see the goodness in your child but end up thinking of her needs and flaws, or of your wishes and hopes for her. Of course, there's no such thing as a perfect child (or perfect parent!), but the point is that if you can think of your child as doing the best that she possibly can given her capabilities, you can develop more compassion for her. Along with compassion, practice gratitude for the child you have.

Starting with acknowledging the difficulty of managing these frustrations, this chapter offered you some specific tools for coping with uncertainty and complexity. The rest of this book equips you with specific knowledge about the autism spectrum, medicine, and education to help you choose as wisely as possible for your child. You are part of the solution, and managing your own tension and thinking is an important aspect of your job as parent. We hope we've been helpful in this regard.

Don't feel bad if all of this seems exhausting! As with any new practice, there's a threshold to overcome; it takes time and energy to learn and implement the approaches in this chapter. But there will be real payoffs. Our advice is to slow down, make a nice cup of tea, sit for five minutes, and slowly breathe in and out. Then get back at it, and know that it will get better.

CHAPTER 5

Getting a Diagnosis

Parents arrive at a diagnosis in different ways. For some, it's a long journey from their initial concern. Foreknowledge and field-tested advice could help. In this chapter, we describe common steps in the process. Along the way, we share suggestions for navigating your interactions with clinicians, administrators, and others you'll work with, now and in the future.

The first step is prompted by a concern. Friends, family members, teachers, or others may suggest that you see an expert. Pediatricians include screening tests for ASDs in checkups (learn more at www.firstsigns.org), and you may get a referral for an appointment. Or, you may seek a specialist because of your own concerns.

We'll discuss physician screening later, but first let's turn to a question many parents ask. How do nonexperts know whether there's cause for concern? This is a tricky area: a diagnosis must be made by a qualified professional. An inexpert opinion could cause a parent to overreact—or to respond defensively and deny the validity of the concerns. We'll share some ideas about how to handle comments by friends, family, and others. Teachers, day care workers, and others who have daily exposure to your child and other children may see things that you do not, and it is their responsibility to alert you to concerns.

For some families, comparisons to siblings provide the first tip-off. But first-time parents may not see indications until they watch their children alongside peers. Playdates, birthday parties, and community events may highlight differences in social interaction, communication, problem solving, or even play skills. In more structured settings, like preschool, music class, or team sports, you may notice that your child is less able to sit still, follow instructions, pay attention appropriately, or answer questions.

Does Your Child Behave Differently?

Being able to describe your child's behavior without rushing to explain it away is a crucial skill for parents of children with autism—one that you will use again and again in your interactions with family members, doctors, teachers, and specialists. If you find yourself coming up with many explanations for why your child does not act like others, use our guidelines to describe observable behavior—what you actually see your child doing—as clearly as possible.

We're not telling you to avoid explaining why your child acts that way. These attributions, which are your own ideas about what is causing the behavior, are valuable too. Just be sure to separate the two.

Practical Note:
Observations and Attributions

It may be easier said than done, but you can cultivate the skill of separating what you observe from what you think. Try it out while watching your child in a group setting. Carefully describe to yourself what you see. If it helps, think of how a researcher would describe what your child is doing. For instance, you might say to yourself, *When the music teacher asks Johnny to name an instrument, he does not answer and does not look at her.*

It's natural to want to explain why; this is called "making attributions." You might think, *Johnny doesn't like his teacher, He didn't get enough sleep last night,* or *I think this is the wrong class for him; we should have signed up for gym class.* Humans are hardwired to explain things, which can be a very useful tendency. But when it comes to sorting out the specific challenges linked to autism, being able to separate what you see from what you think caused it is vitally important; there may be underlying drivers of behavior linked to autism that have nothing to do with the many explanations you can come up with.

Focus on the actual observable behaviors—what other people watching would also see and hear—and take notes. Include as much as you can about the setting and circumstances (location, temperature and noise level, how soon after eating, and so on).

Use these observations when you meet with doctors and specialists. The specifics enable others to better understand your child. Referring to your observations can also help you pinpoint what worries you the most. Carry a notebook, and as you see behaviors that look different from those of your child's peers, jot them down. Gather and review them before your child's next doctor's appointment. You'll be contributing an important piece to the diagnostic puzzle.

When Friends, Family, or Teachers Think Something's Wrong

We mentioned that the first inkling that something's wrong may come from teachers, day care workers, friends, or family. No matter how gentle the delivery, it can be very hard for you to hear this from someone else. And when the bearer of the bad news does not have a style that matches your needs, the experience can be traumatic. It's natural to react defensively when you hear that your child does not appear to be typical. To add to your stress, the other person may not separate his observations from attributions. He may describe specific behaviors to you along with his own view of what the behaviors indicate. As a result, you may be quickly drawn to explaining it away, or he may end up inappropriately labeling what he thinks is wrong with your child.

· Remember to separate observations from attributions. Remind yourself to treat the explanations you are hearing—including a "diagnosis" by a nonmedical professional—as provisional, at best. As you build your own skill in differentiating observation and attribution, you can ask others to do the same. Doing so will equip your family and your team to solve problems more effectively.

Practical Note:
Get It in Writing

When a teacher, friend, or relative gives you unwelcome news about your child, ask for her observations in writing. This is a useful general approach: if you feel that you can't really hear what someone is telling you, feel overwhelmed, or realize that you are reacting defensively, simply tell her that this is valuable information and it would really help to get it in writing, even if it's just a quick e-mail or a short note listing some points. If the report is coming from a teacher or other staff member at a child care center, preschool, or school, a letter is the professional standard. Ask for it.

Handling Screening Tests

We mentioned physician-administered screening tests for young children. They usually involve observations and simple tests, along with some questions for parents during a checkup. Depending on the results, the doctor or nurse may suggest further testing.

A red flag may turn out to be a red herring. If that happens, notice your reaction. You may be grateful that it was nothing, or you may feel angry about the needless worry and wasted time. The thing to remember is that while screens indicate the need for assessment, the screens themselves cannot be used to diagnose. A diagnosis requires specific tests, usually administered by specialists. It's unavoidable in medicine that screening tests sometimes raise concerns that, in the end, turn out to be nothing—that's what screens are for. Because children develop differently, a child who is found not to be on the spectrum at two years of age could receive a diagnosis later on. Conclusions of an early assessment may be reversed later.

We've looked at pediatrician screening tests, your own observations, and feedback from teachers, friends, or family as initial sources that indicate concern. It's possible that other specialists are your first step to a diagnosis—for instance, a speech therapist or your school district's early-intervention team. Regardless of how you get there, once you have the first indications that something is amiss, the formal diagnosis itself is usually made by a specialist. For many families, these diagnostic appointments are the first in many as you work toward a more detailed understanding of your child's profile, challenges, and strengths.

The Diagnostic Appointment

To get a diagnosis, you'll visit one or more of the following professionals: developmental pediatrician, psychologist, speech and language pathologist, neurologist, psychiatrist, neuropsychologist, psychoeducational specialist, or occupational therapist. You may see a diagnostic team or an individual practitioner. Ask about your options.

Setting Up a Diagnostic Appointment

If your child's doctor suggests seeing a specialist, it's a good idea to agree immediately. It may feel like a sensible tactic to wait and see. Resist this idea; the earlier you know, the better for your child. Make the most of any help to set up an appointment right away.

If you are offered a referral, immediately ask about the logistics. If your health care provider requires additional steps or paperwork, ask how you can help speed things along. Even at this early stage, there may be other sources of help that you need to start lining up; for example, you may be authorized to see a medical social worker. Someone who specializes in managing complex cases can be a godsend for your family.

Practical Note:
Getting an Appointment

One of your earliest challenges may be unexpected: the waiting list. In some areas, an appointment with a specialist entails weeks or months of delay. Some practices are closed to new patients. But the evidence is strongly against waiting. At this point, consider some parent-tested tactics for getting off the waiting list:

- Get on multiple waiting lists, even if you do not intend to see several specialists. As soon as you get in to see one, cancel the others. Do not use this strategy if you're not well organized; avoid having to cancel an appointment at the last moment or, worse, forgetting to go to one.

- Tell the scheduler your child's age; the younger the child, the higher the priority, in many cases. Have your pediatrician or family doctor call on your behalf too.

- Check for cancellations. If there are none, ask (nicely, of course) what day and time would be convenient for you to call back. If your schedule permits, let the scheduler know that you could make a last-minute appointment. Provide multiple ways to contact you, making it easy for the person to reach you if there's an opening. And if you are available around Thanksgiving or another holiday, let the office know; there may be unexpected openings then.

- Negotiate with the specialist. You may be able to convince her to come in early or stay late to squeeze in an appointment. Consider rearranging your own schedule for this first appointment.

- Be speedy with the paperwork. Turn in any forms right away, with a friendly note attached, and ensure that information from your child's doctor or insurer arrives as needed.

One father made a point of personally bringing in promptly completed paperwork. His hand-delivery method helped to build a relationship with office staff, demonstrated commitment, and allowed him to figure out how to get there, where to park, and what the logistics would be—all useful for his own planning and for helping to manage his son's anxiety. Of course, this works only if you have a flexible schedule and getting to the office is not too inconvenient!

Whom to See, If You Have a Choice

When your child's doctor refers your child for diagnosis, inquire about the options for whom to see. Jog his memory by asking whether he recalls any specialist reports he particularly admires.

Because the professions abide by common diagnostic criteria, in theory any qualified professional should make the same diagnosis, regardless of specialization. In practice, different types of doctors and medical professionals tend to focus on different things and have different ideas about treatment. You cannot know at the outset which specialist's approach will be best for your child. If you have a choice, a commonsense strategy is to see the specialist most recommended by others.

As you explore options, realize that the specialist or team who diagnoses your child may not be involved in ongoing care. You may drive hours to a hospital with a developmental pediatric clinic to get your child diagnosed, never to visit it again because it's not practical to do so.

Should you get a second opinion? If it's feasible, consider seeing multiple specialists. Each paints a picture of your child, helping you better understand her specific issues, while also giving you a chance to learn about work styles, how the practice operates, and the specialty field. Every conversation that you have with a specialist is a chance to learn something, whether it's about brain development, the physiological aspects of toilet training, or using reinforcements effectively. Look at every appointment as a learning opportunity.

A drawback to the second-opinion approach is that each expert may give you a *different* picture of the challenges and next steps for your child. If you tend to get overwhelmed with information, seeing two experts could cause more stress than benefit. If you do go to different experts, work with your team to figure out what to make of the various reports. Later chapters offer you practical advice on managing specialists with this issue in mind.

The reality for many families is that location, health care payment options, and availability dictate who diagnoses your child, putting the question of whom to see out of your hands. If you're like other parents of children with autism, over the years you will end up interacting with a variety of specialists, and the specific orientation of the person who makes your child's diagnosis fades in importance over time. More important is the person's skill, which is why we suggest asking your child's doctors and others for recommendations.

Don't despair if early encounters with specialists feel difficult. This is new to you, after all. The specialists you first see may not have interpersonal styles that fit your needs. Realize that the skills that make a good diagnostician are not always those of an excellent caregiver or therapist. A pediatric neurologist who conducts laboratory research may be stellar in that specialty, but may not be the right person to work with on an ongoing basis. Knowing that you have time in the months ahead to assemble a team that works for you on an ongoing basis may make it easier to handle the specialists you encounter at this stage. Some parents spend months looking for "Dr. Perfect," only to realize that no single specialist can manage all aspects of their child's care. It has to be a team, as we'll explain.

Practical Note:
Preparing for the Diagnostic Appointment

Once you have the appointment, start preparing. Ask whether you will be seeing a team (for example, in a hospital clinic) or an individual; find out whether the diagnosis entails multiple appointments or just one. Manage the administrative details: call the office, ask for paperwork (if your child hates waiting, you may want to complete forms at home) and directions. Print out maps and ask how much time you should allow for the journey from the parking garage or bus stop to the clinic door. Ask whether appointments tend to run late and what you should plan on. Be nice to the staff, because in return, when the time comes, they may help you out; for instance, if you end up having to wait, they may agree to call you when you're next, allowing you to walk the hallways with your child. As the appointment draws near, gather comforting toys and books for your child, plenty of preferred snacks, and anything else that helps keep your child calm or comforted.

Make sure that you bring notes describing the aspects of your child's behavior that are most concerning. We mentioned the importance of distinguishing between observations and attributions. The doctor uses your descriptions to develop a picture of your child's functioning.

Consider who should come to the appointment. Do you need a notetaker? Should you bring a family member or friend who is skilled at clarifying complicated or confusing situations to help facilitate the interaction? Should you bring someone to sit with your child in the waiting room or keep him busy if there is a delay? Not only do you need to figure out whom you would like to join you at the appointment, but you also should talk it over with that person ahead of time. Most supporters are happy to be given a clear task.

When the day of your appointment comes, make sure you have your notebook. As you wait to go in, ask for the names of every person you are seeing (you may not want to do this on the way out), noting everyone's specialty, title, or role. Don't forget to note names of the receptionist and other staff.

Make sure you already know what you want *after* the appointment. Often a consultation report is sent from the specialist to the referring doctor. You'll ask for a copy of the report, but also consider who else needs to see this report and how it will be used. You may need an official diagnosis to qualify for special services from your school district or to secure coverage for specific services from your insurer. The more you know about how others will use the report, the better equipped you are to ask for what you need.

The formal consultation apart, it can also help to get session notes immediately after the appointment. This is less likely an option if you are seeing an individual, but if you see a team, one of them may be able to send you the notes. The value of this approach becomes apparent when you learn that many specialists take longer (*months* longer) than you'd expect to produce a report. Part of your preparation is to figure out your required timing: how soon is it needed? Knowing this timing is useful in discussing and confirming next steps with the specialist, and while you wait, the notes can help you start your own next steps.

The Appointment Itself

What happens during the diagnostic appointment depends on your child as well as the experts' specialties and their preferred set of tests. You will spend some time talking to one or more experts. Don't be surprised if you're asked questions you've already answered in writing or you're asked to recount details that seem remote or irrelevant to you. Many of these questions are standard, and over the years you will likely be asked them over and over again!

When you are asked to describe your child's behaviors, respond as "scientifically" as you can. Try to set aside what you want the diagnosis to be or what you fear it might be. Your job as a parent, when you're wrestling with a diagnostic puzzle, is to give the experts the most accurate and complete information—not the information that leads toward the diagnosis you *think* you want!

Your child will take tests. Some will feel like play, while others may require continuing until she fails a given number of times in a row. Such tests are not designed to make you—or your child—feel good, and you might notice that you take your child's difficulties personally. Getting upset when you observe that your child can't complete tasks or exhibit skills that you suspect are easy for typical kids won't help you or your child in the evaluation.

The Diagnosis

You may or may not be given the results immediately. Some specialists deliver the diagnosis in a separate follow-up appointment. This has the advantage of taking place without your child but the disadvantage of requiring you to wait longer. Realize that many specialists are not expert at addressing your feelings in the moment and that their attempts to reassure you may fall short. Actually hearing the diagnosis can be difficult, even if you are expecting it.

Along with the diagnosis, you may be offered help. It's possible that the offer won't make sense in the moment. Why would your child need an occupational therapist? What can a trainee speech pathologist do? At this point, you may be in information overload, realizing that there is much you need to learn. Don't write off anything at this early point; get the information, and say you'll get back to the person. If it's possible, make a plan ahead of time for what you will do directly afterward to process what you have learned. What would help you? Time alone or with others?

And now, as you finally narrow in on your child's overall diagnosis— one that puts him somewhere on the autism spectrum—your next task is to piece together a profile of your child.

CHAPTER 6

Understanding Your Child's Specifics and Building Your Treatment Team

Y ou have the official diagnosis. Perhaps it's been a struggle to get here: a trail of paperwork, waiting lists, and appointments ending with news you'd hoped against. And now, as you absorb what you've learned, you may be questioning what the future holds for you, your child, and your family.

And you may be realizing that a diagnosis can't tell you everything. What does your child most need? How will she learn? What's most important for her participation in the world? Some of these are big questions that can't be answered easily, but you will want to start working on things right away because treatment can't wait. For many parents, the next step is a round of more detailed assessments.

What? More Tests?

If you're lucky, the diagnostic process equipped you with what's needed to plan the next steps. If your child saw a diagnostic team, you may now have detailed assessments and recommendations in speech and language, occupational and physical therapy, social skills, and academics. This information equips you to set up treatment from an early-intervention program, negotiate for therapies from your health care provider, or work with your child's school on an educational plan.

More often, families learn that they must dig deeper to understand more specifics. Maybe you suspect that your child has tactile issues, but is he oversensitive or undersensitive to touch? Two children with an autism diagnosis may have very different profiles. One boy doesn't notice that he puts his shirts on backward. He doesn't seem to care if the shirt tag tickles his throat and, on a cold winter day, may leave the house underdressed and not appear to notice. Another child in the same family may refuse to wear entire categories of clothes: no collars, ever. He insists on knit hats almost year-round. The tags on his clothes have all been removed.

When it comes to clothing, it's relatively clear what the issues are. Other challenges are more subtle but can have huge effects.

Why You Need to Understand Your Child's Profile

Consider a first grader who didn't seem to pay attention in class. Suggesting that he lacked concentration, his teacher proposed a reward system to reinforce desired classroom behavior. The teacher planned to place an aide behind him to tap his shoulder whenever he should be looking ahead at the teacher. The child would be taught challenging materials outside the classroom.

His parents were puzzled. At home, their son seemed to have amazing concentration. Did he lack motivation? But they didn't know how to motivate a young child, especially one who had his own interests and created his own complex projects at home. Rewards didn't seem to drive him. But they couldn't think of anything else. So the teacher's plan seemed reasonable, and they went along with it.

Now consider what happened when the parents sought to better understand their son's profile. An expert in sensory integration (SI) and a neuropsychologist each assessed the boy. Both found that he had difficulty separating certain background sounds from foreground sounds. In an observational visit, the SI expert pointed out that the classroom overlooked a city street. Throughout the day, traffic noise varied in pitch and intensity. This varying background sound required exactly the sort of auditory filtering that was most difficult for the boy. Perhaps he could be seated farther from the windows? The SI expert also suggested listening therapy at home to improve his auditory filtering.

An occupational therapist assessed the boy, finding weak trunk strength. At home, the child moved around freely, sitting in whatever way he found comfortable. At school, he was supposed to sit in a certain way. Doing so took effort for the first grader, making everything else he was supposed to do at the same time—like paying attention to the teacher—extra difficult. No wonder it was tough for him to concentrate! The occupational therapist recommended a footrest to reduce the physical demand of sitting in a hard, armless school chair, and worked on trunk-strengthening exercises with him in weekly sessions.

These insights led to changes that helped the boy do better at school. Notice that the experts proposed adaptations—move his seat, add a footrest—and provided therapies to address weaknesses. The parents also learned from these steps. Not only did they understand more about their son, but also they learned about the process. In particular, it was important for them to be able to help test others' attributions in ways that were constructive and collaborative. They agreed to the interventions that the teacher proposed, but they also asked whether they could bring in an SI specialist and the child's occupational therapist to observe him at school.

The lesson is that when you develop an accurate picture of your child's specific strengths and weaknesses, you can define and advocate for the most appropriate therapies and accommodations.

How to Develop a Profile of Your Child's Strengths and Weaknesses

Like many steps on your parenting journey, this isn't a one-time task but an ongoing process. Your options will change over time: your child will develop and grow, therapies will have their effect, and new treatments and supports will become available. At the same time, you face constraints. Your time, money, and energy permit only a subset of all possible evaluations. Start to build a picture of your child's sensory, physical, language, and cognitive profile, knowing that it will be evolving and incomplete. As you encounter experts in different areas, your interactions will help you learn more. As we pointed out earlier, not only do you obtain useful information from experts' formal assessments and recommendations, but also you glean new insights and add to your understanding via conversations and meetings and by sitting in on sessions.

Both formal and informal information is useful. We suggest keeping a portfolio of formal reports along with e-mails and notes from your interactions with specialists. Use these materials to prepare overviews of your child's profile to share whenever your child makes a transition.

The Experts and Their Approaches

Now, who can help build your child's profile? A speech and language pathologist (SLP), also known as a speech therapist, is essential for identifying your child's language strengths and weaknesses and for setting goals. Your team uses the profile and goals to define a treatment plan and strategies for supporting your child's participation in school and elsewhere.

An expert in sensory integration and an occupational therapist (who may or may not be the same person) will help you understand the physical and sensory issues and how to both accommodate and treat them. A physical therapist identifies and addresses poor physical function with exercises and physical treatments.

A neuropsychologist or a neurologist can help you understand how your child's brain and neurological system work. This professional's focus may overlap with that of an occupational therapist or SI specialist, regarding auditory or visual processing, for instance. She can also help you understand cognitive strengths and weaknesses. Translating her findings into specifics for school and home is another step: some specialists are very strong in this area, but in other cases you may need other team members to help figure out the therapies and specific supports that are most needed.

An educational psychologist or a neuropsychologist can help you understand how the cognitive aspects of your child's profile affect academic performance, as well as recommend specific skills, interests, and strengths to build on for learning.

Academic and other specialists who are trained to assess and help children with autism in specific areas are useful; for instance, the Lindamood-Bell Learning Processes involve assessing certain communication skills, which in turn dictates a treatment program. For specific programs like this one, assessments are tied to the treatment, which means that you must sign up for the whole package to get the most from it. Other assessments and instructional programs with embedded data collection are designed for all children or for learning-disabled children. Some programs are facilitated by trained teachers or therapists, but other programs can be used by families on their own. One example is IXL (www.ixl.com), a kid-friendly math site that automatically collects data every time your child uses it, providing handy reports you can share with your child's school.

Experts in social skills and social facilitation may administer specific assessments and help devise a treatment plan focused on social interaction.

Developmental, educational, and behavioral experts have developed a variety of evidence-based assessment tools. For example, the Assessment of Basic Language and Learning Skills (ABLLS) is an applied behavior analysis (ABA) framework for measuring gaps in language, academic, self-help, and motor skills. It's tied to an ABA approach for implementing and monitoring intervention. Almost every educational approach that we describe later in this book involves specialized assessments designed to give you a global picture of your child. In some cases, certified consultants conduct the assessment and come up with a plan. The team behind SCERTS, an approach described in chapter 10, published comprehensive manuals to guide you through assessment and connect you to relevant interventions and goals (Prizant et al. 2005).

But you can't do everything! This is why we think it's essential that you partner with a professional. Together you can guide your child's treatment. We've gathered some practical ideas for managing your team of doctors and specialists. Finding the clinician to serve as your partner is your first task.

Building the Right Treatment Team

Once you build a relationship with one medical expert, you'll have a partner to help you decide whom to turn to for further diagnostic information and assessments so you can build a picture of your child's needs. Your partner will help you interpret results, shaping your early choices about your child's treatment. Later, this expert will help you reassess your child's progress and needs.

Why is a partner so important? It's up to you to build your team of treatment experts, but you could likely use some guidance, because you may find yourself confronting many options for treatment. Do you address anxiety with a visit to a psychopharmacologist? A behavioral therapist? A sensory integration specialist? A psychologist? Not surprisingly, each specialist will orient you toward an approach in line with her training. To the parent of a newly diagnosed child, every decision can seem overwhelming; so much seems to ride on the choice of the specialist, and then more rides on the decisions that ensue.

A partner with a medical professional background can help you choose whom to see, what to try, and what to make of the reports and results that follow. But it's your job to help define the role this expert plays. You'll need to evaluate whether she is the right partner for you.

Partnering with Your Child's Doctor

As you move beyond diagnosis, your child's present doctor could be your guide and traveling companion along the way—or may simply send you off. Is it time to wave good-bye and find a new partner for this stage of your parenting journey?

Your child's doctor acts as a gatekeeper of sorts, thanks to the way that many HMOs and insurance plans work. He is the source of all-important referrals to specialists, without which specialist fees may not be covered, so there are financial implications for you. He may choose, or at least agree to, the specific specialists you consult. When your child needs more treatment than is normally covered under your plan—say, occupational therapy sessions beyond the program's limit—your pediatrician can appeal to the plan's oversight committee or board for an exemption. This gatekeeper role is important.

Another important function is the overall guidance of your child's medical care. This is one of the main jobs of any pediatrician or family doctor. In the case of a child with autism, the guidance role is complex. A routine check for levels of lead in the blood is even more important for a child with a developmental delay, but sensory, anxiety, or cognitive challenges may make drawing blood impossible. Ensuring that your child gets all the regular medical care she needs might take some extra creativity and perseverance.

But the overall guidance goes beyond routine care. A doctor treating a child with autism should ensure that the family consult experts and examine issues that they may be unaware of. Many families may not think of going to a geneticist, unless they are contemplating having another child, but genetic testing could reveal conditions that look very similar to autism, such as Rett's disorder or fragile X syndrome, for which treatment and prognoses may vary.

Doctors can also help you broaden the range of options to consider and then choose wisely among them. An eight-year-old who wets the bed could visit a neurologist to be prescribed an evening medication that stops urination or could see a behavioral therapist for a program to wake up the child to visit the bathroom at lengthening intervals. Alternatively, parents could skip the experts and head to the store for underwear-style diapers. Which approach works? It all depends, but a pediatrician or family doctor who injects perspective and guidance into the family's choices can make life easier for everyone.

Pediatricians or family doctors can also connect you with support groups and other parents who've made the same journey you're on, and they can alert you to community events and resources. They may contribute a complementary perspective to your child's school-based team. When things are contentious, this can be particularly helpful. Even if it's infeasible for a doctor to come to your child's school or attend official team meetings, his input can be a great source of support and encouragement. Some parents set up quick conversations with their child's doctor at key points in the educational planning process. Touching base provides a useful sanity check.

Pediatricians interact with schools, summer camps, and other organizations when they complete required medical forms. Your child's doctor can note the special supports—and document relevant skills and capabilities—that enable you to argue for specific accommodations or opportunities for your child.

You can also work with your child's doctor to make things more efficient. For instance, some medications require frequent visits to the prescribing doctor, but going to see a specialist, such as a pediatric psychopharmacologist, every few months can be time consuming and expensive. One solution is to work with the specialist for a period of time while you are charting a course of action and then, once you have a program that works well, switch to seeing your pediatrician for a period, returning to the specialist as needed but getting the prescriptions from your pediatrician the rest of the time.

No doctor is perfect, but as we've suggested, now may be the right time to consider whether you have the right one for your needs. Even if you have no choice in this matter, it may still be helpful to assess the doctor in order to get a sense of what help you might need to seek elsewhere.

Practical Note:
Checklist for Choosing Your Child's Doctor

☐ Does she have much experience with autism? Is she interested in it?

☐ Does she know what expertise is needed? Does she know that there are likely things outside her knowledge base?

☐ Does she have a wide professional network? Would she track down a needed connection—say, to find the best expert in facilitated communication?

☐ Will she educate her peers and other medical professionals about what she is learning with you?

☐ Does she have time for you? Can she offer longer appointments? Would she meet with you to talk through a difficult decision?

☐ Can her practice accommodate your child's sensory and other needs? Some offer children with autism the first slot of the day; offices are quieter, delays are less likely, and the child benefits from consistent timing and predictability in his experience of the visit. Some will place your child in the quietest room or one where his tendency to make a lot of noise won't be a problem.

☐ Will the doctor go the extra mile in figuring out how to get your child needed medical care? For instance, will she research probiotic supplements or track down separate doses for vaccines that are usually combined, if that is something that you all agree is important?

☐ Is the practice prompt with paperwork? Do you think the doctor would "go to bat" against the HMO or someone else, should such a need arise, to argue on your child's behalf?

☐ What do others have to say about the doctor?

If You Need to Change: Finding a New Pediatrician

If you need to find a new doctor, we have some suggestions. Use the checklist as a guide. For instance, you may want to track down a pediatrician with autism spectrum experience. One parent called the medical director of her HMO and got a list of the pediatricians most interested in working with children on the spectrum. Or you may wish to seek the advice of other parents, whether in support groups, waiting rooms, or online forums.

If you think you need some skilled help in your search, ask your insurance plan or HMO whether you can work with a medical social worker; these specialists can do useful research, tracking down sources of data and information that can help you uncover more options. And they will meet with you to strategize and plan your course of action, thereby helping solve the immediate problem while teaching you skills in case management that you will need again in the future. Patient advocates can also be great and serve as free resources if you run into trouble.

When you think you've found a good candidate, interview him. Pediatricians are accustomed to informational interviews and should handle such meetings with professionalism. Realize that no doctor will be able to do everything you wish for, and he may be operating under conditions that limit his flexibility. You may need to draw on others to meet some of the needs that we've listed, and that can be a perfectly fine—or even great—solution for your family.

Practical Note:
When the Relationship with Your Child's Doctor Does Not Work

Sometimes the relationship just does not work. Here are some suggestions for separating from your child's doctor:

- If you are changing doctors, remember that you might still need reports and information from your current one. Don't "fire" your child's doctor while angry!

- An open, honest dialogue helps both sides learn. Ideally, you'd let the doctor know what has not worked; issues usually involve communication, follow-up, timeliness of reports, and so on.

- The treatment community might be small. Your child's new doctor's practice may end up contacting your old one. Take the high road when discussing doctors and other professionals with other people.

- Use a natural transition, such as the end of the school year or vacations, as a time to move on.

During your transition, make sure you continue to track daily records and gather medical information for your next doctor.

Who Else Could Play This Role?

We discussed how to partner with your pediatrician, general practitioner, or family doctor in managing your child's overall program. Are there other options for this role? Although you may not return to the person or team of experts who diagnosed your child, in some cases an expert such as a developmental pediatrician both diagnoses and treats. It can be an advantage for a specialist to play this dual role. It's much less depressing to hear bad news about your child's diagnosis from someone who has treated similar children who improved, and things can get started more quickly when the diagnosing doctor or team initiates treatment. This is the idea behind multidisciplinary clinics.

Another candidate is a neurologist who is interested in autism and children. Neurologists look for co-occurring conditions and issues, and they seek to identify any underlying conditions, such as Landau-Kleffner syndrome (chapter 2). Neurologists may see their patients on an ongoing basis, so your regular visits could potentially serve as a checkup on your child's overall condition, program, and prognosis. If your child has some neurological condition besides autism, you may see a neurologist regularly, especially if treatment entails medication. In many cases, however, neurologists do not manage ongoing care. Alternatively, a psychiatrist whom your child visits regularly may take a similar oversight role.

One benefit of partnering with a developmental specialist, neurologist, or psychiatrist interested in ASDs is that this type of professional may be following emerging research on autism more closely. This person can be your fast track to new ideas and information, helping you interpret new findings. In any case, to assess the potential fit with your needs, you'll want to run through the checklist questions previously noted.

As you line up your partner and your team, take this opportunity to map out how you will make every appointment work best for you and your child.

Making Every Appointment Effective

Whether you have a routine appointment with your child's pediatrician or a first-time visit to a specialist, your preparation can make a big difference. Consider reviewing the practical suggestions presented in chapter 5, which can help with any appointment, not just the diagnostic ones. We turned the advice into a quick list for you to use again and again, incorporating some additional helpful ideas, such as the suggestion to keep a "hot list" that tracks the issues your family considers most important at the moment. Focusing on your top concerns instead of the universe of all possible issues can make even the most difficult times easier to manage.

Practical Note:
Five Habits for a Highly Effective Appointment

Parents and doctors alike tell us that even quick preparation for an appointment is better than none. Here are five habits to cultivate.

Master the logistics and paperwork for a first visit. Call the office. You may need directions and payment information. Also, ask:

- What paperwork can be completed ahead of time

- What kind of information to bring (what's required, what would be helpful: videos, daily logs?)

- Whether you may bring a notetaker or record the appointment for your own use

- How long to expect the appointment to last (including realistic delays)

- After the appointment, how long any written report might take

- For an e-mail address where you can send a follow-up note

Know what you want to come out of this appointment. Sometimes you seek advice or help in reaching a decision. Other times, you may visit a doctor to validate and discuss your concerns. Or your objectives may be more concrete: a referral or prescription, a form to be completed, a written report to be produced within a given time frame.

Be clear in your mind about what you need or are asking for. Talk it over with someone. If you're asking for something difficult, practice your request so that it's easier to do in the moment.

Prepare your agenda. Make an agenda based on your family's hot list of urgent concerns regarding your child, arranged with your most pressing concern at the top. Narrow down the list to three to five issues, and print out copies to share and use. Leave space for notes.

Gather, organize, and bring data. Doctors tell us that often parents are not that clear in reporting concerns; even a little data can be very helpful. For instance, if sleep is an issue, log the number of hours your child sleeps; if your child self-injures, you might want to videotape the behavior. Other things to log include eating, going to the toilet, and any moods you are concerned about. Bring along observational notes (your own, teachers', or others).

Follow up and check that you're on the same page. Go over what happened at the appointment, and plan to send a brief follow-up e-mail or note to summarize what you learned and any next steps.

Preparing for every appointment sets you up to be a more effective partner with the clinician. Having concerns, ideas, and data lined up is an excellent way to ensure that your input is taken into account. You also signal to the professional that you value her time and expertise, which puts you on good footing for collaborating on complex challenges. It can even help you cultivate your own sense of authority, so that when you ask some of the difficult questions we've laid out in the following chapters, you may feel a bit more confident in doing so.

We know that spending time gathering data and writing agendas is much less fun than watching a TV show or getting a little more sleep, but it will pay off in the long run. Think of it like flossing your teeth: it's something that you just do. If you can build your own set of habits for preparing before and following up after each appointment, things will be easier down the road. You'll make the most of the money, effort, and time you spend at doctor's appointments—and help ensure better care for your child too.

CHAPTER 7

Choosing Interventions and Treatments

Parents of children with autism have tried heavy metal chelation, Reiki therapy, elimination diets, facilitated communication, music therapy, applied behavior analysis, prescription psychiatric medications, hyperbaric oxygen treatments, acupuncture, speech and language therapy, reverse integration at school, therapy dogs, and neurofeedback. And that's just a start.

You may be wondering whether all of these options even belong on the same list. Some are treatments, some are interventions or therapies, and some accommodate and assist rather than cure. Yet these distinctions can be misleading. For a developmental disorder like autism, there's no cure, but interventions can have therapeutic effects. You may aspire to choose from all feasible options, but too often, the information is divided into categories that make it difficult to compare. As part of our integrated view of autism, this chapter provides what we consider to be one of our most useful tools: a practical guide for sorting through treatment options and deciding what to do—and what not to do.

We'll use the terms "treatment" and "intervention" interchangeably, drawing on ideas presented throughout this book. Rather than explain every treatment, we will give you a broad overview of our practical approach to the array of options and suggest strategies for organizing your approach to decisions. By the end, you'll be equipped to consider a wide range of choices presented in the remaining chapters, along with new ones that will emerge in the years to come.

Learn about Providers and What They Do

We've discussed specialists who help develop your child's profile and diagnosis. As you consider treatments and interventions, the specialists who may provide them are a good place to start our guide to the selection process.

A Provider's Orientation Matters

Everyone tends to see the world through the lens of their own experience and training. Physicians, educators, and therapists are no exception. As a result, you may get different advice from different experts. Before you knock on any doors, get a sense of the domains where the experts reside. In some cases, professional qualifications provide the tip-off: an MD who is board certified in pediatrics tends to take a medical and developmental view, and rely on research studies and guidelines from the national professional organization (in the United States, the American Academy of Pediatrics). This type of doctor may know little about bodywork and energy therapies. Osteopaths and chiropractors are also doctors but are likely to emphasize nontraditional interventions.

Those letters after a professional's name—BCBA, CCC-SLP—tell you that the person is versed in core areas of his discipline and has met certification criteria. Descriptions of the purview of each type of certified therapist can help you set your expectations in working with one. You can find this information online; for instance, the website of the Behavior Analyst Certification Board (bacb.com) explains what behavioral therapists do. Ethical standards and shared goals of each profession are also laid out in its association's materials and equip you to inquire about how your child's specialist is meeting these standards, should the need arise. If you are in a position to choose providers, use our checklist for choosing a doctor in chapter 6 to get the most from your initial conversations with specialists.

Every Specialist and Therapist Works Differently

Professionals with the same qualifications differ in personal style and philosophy. Experience, expertise, and interest in specific treatments and therapies vary. Some occupational therapists emphasize sensory issues, treating with deep pressure, skin brushing, and spinning, while others teach specific skills like bike riding. And the school itself, or other institutional setting, may shape providers' approaches, either formally, via job descriptions, or through shared assumptions about what each specialist should or should not do. Therapists who look the same on paper may practice very differently.

In some areas of need, different providers work on the same thing. Social interaction is an obvious example: a speech therapist pairs your child with a peer for coaching in conversational skills. In group occupational therapy sessions, your child's occupational therapist works on turn taking, a core element of social interaction. And in the classroom, your child's teacher structures opportunities to practice and develop social interaction skills via real-time guidance and feedback during a group science experiment.

Look at Needs and Goals First, Not Providers

Different specialists' work can overlap, and the same goals can be worked on at home, in school, in special sessions, and in the community. In some ways, this complicates your job: you can't just check off boxes to define your child's treatment program. We recommend starting with the developments you most want for your child, using these goals to choose or refine your team of specialists. The process is iterative: you learn by talking and working with specialists, and this helps you refine your understanding of your child's needs and potential for development, which in turn informs how you shape his program.

Practical Note:
Get Smart about the Grid

Some parents of newly diagnosed children fall into the trap of shopping from a list of specialists, but the school's education plan also has pitfalls. As the school plans for your child's treatment, administrators may go straight to negotiating how many hours of a given service your child will get every week. This list of time commitments by each type of personnel—laid out in a "service delivery grid"—specifies key details of your child's individualized educational program (commonly referred to as IEP), the formal agreement defining your child's school, and possibly outside-school, program. It's important because it codifies what your child will receive beyond the regular school program, but focusing on the grid first is problematic because it directs attention to the minutes per week that a given expert will work with your child, not to the developments you would most like your child to reach.

There's an inescapable truth: even the best school or specialist cannot guarantee that your child will reach a given development. On the other hand, you can advocate for your child more effectively if you know that a potential trap is to focus on the minutes per week of various services rather than on what the specialists will teach or develop in your child. Sometimes you need to push the team to discuss in more depth what changes they aim to develop in your child, even if this means adding a step before discussing the specifics of your child's plan and the grid.

Navigate the Terrain of Treatments and Interventions

So, providers are important, but needs and goals are even more important in selecting treatments. Your job is to ensure the best match between your child's needs and her overall program of treatments. To take care of the first part, you developed a detailed profile of your child's needs with your team as you worked through the previous chapter. Before you consider matches between your child's needs and program, you need a sense of the second part of the equation: the treatment and intervention options. To help you navigate the landscape of these options, let's see if we can help organize your thinking without oversimplifying things or inundating you with details.

Categorizing Interventions

The five-part framework followed in this book provides a starting point. Medical interventions (chapter 8) fall into one group. Other interventions that affect the body form the biomedical, physical, and sensory category (chapter 9). Educational approaches (chapter 10) provide another set of interventions, and then there are the techniques that focus on social, communication, and language needs (chapter 11). Interventions that build your child's ability to get by in the world (chapter 12) form our final category.

Practical Note:
Balance the Mix

A big-picture view may help you consider the overall balance of your efforts in these categories. Are you looking only at one type of treatment or intervention at the expense of others? For example, you can separate everything that's traditional from alternative options. If you are looking only at conventional treatments, maybe you should consider adding an alternative intervention too.

Another way to characterize options is by their attention to underlying causes. Some treatments and interventions address physical causes thought to give rise to autism: specialized diets and supplements, for example, aim to change the body and thereby affect behavior. Others tackle symptoms, physical capabilities, or behaviors, aiming only to create directly observable change.

Alternatively, you could differentiate those interventions that address the body—massage, medication, supplements, sensory integration therapies—from those that focus on behaviors and thinking, such as teaching and speech and language therapy.

For parents, perhaps the biggest distinction among treatments involves evidence. When it comes to treating autism, how do you separate what is known to work from what remains unproven?

The Role of Evidence

Medical experts talk about their "gold standard" for figuring out what works. Here's how they put it: only prospectively randomized, double-blind, placebo-controlled trials with sufficient sample sizes and follow-up windows can establish efficacy (see chapter 8). We remain far from this standard when it comes to most autism interventions.

Absent solid evidence regarding treatments, it's easy for ideas that *sound* plausible to catch on. When they spread—even when news about them spreads—that itself can create the impression of validity, as journalists write stories, television shows feature them, "tweets" pile up, blog posts magnify the buzz, and books extol their value. When your aunt sends you newspaper clippings and web links about the latest treatment and the same topic comes up in the online discussion forum you follow, it's hard not to think that there's something to it.

Cultivate an appropriate skepticism by remembering that anecdotal evidence isn't enough. No matter how compelling and vivid it sounds, and no matter how high its listing on a search-engine results page, a one-off case, small and time-limited study, or intriguing hypothesis isn't evidence.

But a lack of evidence does not mean you should rule it out. There may be something to it, after all!

Practical Note:
Be Open to the Unproven along with the Proven

Start with appropriate, evidence-based interventions. Your child's medical specialists and other experts—often the diagnosing physician or team—make formal recommendations for interventions that form the basis of your child's program. Not only do such recommended treatments tend to be clinically validated, but also their costs are most likely to be covered by school districts or health plans. Schools and doctors are expected to hew to the evidence base when it comes to selecting treatments for your child. If you end up disagreeing with your school system, it's the evidence-based arguments that are likely to hold sway. You'll want to ground what you do in evidence wherever it makes sense to do so.

Many parents go beyond the evidence base to include unconventional therapies and interventions. This is not necessarily a bad thing. Medicine and science progress by the slow accumulation of results. Before there was sufficient evidence to support them, treatments now regarded as acceptable by the establishment were once unproven and unconventional. So just because something is not proven does not mean it is useless. And we don't have time for the needed results to roll in. Evidence for or against interventions for autism will continue to accumulate only slowly, for reasons already mentioned.

So, we suggest keeping an open mind when it comes to unproven interventions. At the same time, you already know that you can't possibly look into, let alone try out, every possible treatment and intervention. Some could waste your time and money. Others could even harm your child. What you need is some practical help in making choices.

Make Your Choice

Now that you know more about providers and are learning to map the range of various treatment options, how will you choose what to do—and what not to do? Even figuring out what options to consider may seem daunting. Our three-part guide is designed to help you identify what's most important, learn more about each option, and check that it works for your family. We'll take you through this process, step by step.

Identify What's Important for Your Child

Start by focusing on what's most important for your child and your family.

Practical Note:
Select Your Priorities

As you select treatments and interventions to consider using, three questions can help guide your thinking by highlighting what's most important for your child and your family:

- *What is the change we would like for our child?*

- *What is the behavior we currently observe?*

- *What's most important to us?*

Draw on the practical ideas outlined next to come up with your answers to these three questions.

Identify the desired change. Start by clarifying what you seek to change or enable for your child. Carefully describe your child's problems or needs. Check the importance of each issue by discussing your ideas with your family, team, and child, if appropriate. Make sure to include needs, gaps in skills and abilities, and opportunities so that you are trying not only to eliminate problems but also to spur development and to make the most of emerging abilities and interests. The goal is to specify the changes you most want to enable in your child.

Describe the presentation. If it's a problem, start by describing the specific behavior. Write a short, concrete, and specific statement that lists what anyone watching would observe.

If you are looking at a need or developmental goal instead of a problem, you may have to think carefully. Broad developmental goals can be difficult to sum up in a concrete description. One suggestion is to use a specific behavior as a proxy for a larger set of desired developments. For instance, to tap into needed language, social, and cognitive skills and developments, you could list some specific situations in which your child does not ask questions but it would be helpful for him to do so. If you set a goal for him to ask such questions spontaneously, the corresponding interventions are likely to support development in the broader areas.

Establish priority. Talk to your family, team, and others to assess the size and impact of the concern. One parent may consider her child's hand flapping a problem, but if the rest of the team thinks it's not hampering the child's development, they may place it lower on the list. At the same time, as a parent, you are entitled to address things that burden you more than they do others. Your teenaged son may be unconcerned about his bedwetting, but you are sick of changing the sheets. The issue is more yours than his, but it could make sense to put it at the top of your list when you factor in his needs and yours.

Include developmental effects in your prioritization. Ask whether the proposed goal would, in turn, support subsequent participation, learning, and development.

This process yields a list of goals that factor in both developmental needs and family priorities. Bring the entire list to meetings with specialists, because some interventions and treatments target multiple concerns. But the top item provides your focus and defines the change that you consider most important for your child. It could involve any domain. Here are some examples: "We want Monique to stop all self-injurious behavior," "We want Connor to participate more fully in class discussions," "We want José to be less anxious when encountering changes in routines," and "We want Rita to sleep through the night."

Learn about the Interventions

With the leading issue as your focus, generate a list of approaches to explore. Consult the Internet, other parents, your team, and books for suggestions. As you learn more about your options, you'll discover that some are infeasible. A world-famous specialist may charge hundreds of dollars per hour—out of your price range. The only place that offers therapeutic horse riding in your part of the country may have a two-year waiting list. There may not be a hyperbaric oxygen chamber within driving distance. You may also find that some options are unappealing: even if a human interaction program involving swimming with dolphins is feasible, your own personal concerns about the mammals' treatment may rule it out. Settle on a short list of options that are, at least in theory, feasible for you.

Practical Note:
Understanding Potential Treatments

Now consider each potential treatment or intervention. Information is available in the library, online, or from meeting with experts. Your child's primary doctor may be able to answer questions. Some health plans and other organizations offer access to online databases that have been vetted by experts and written specifically for patients—a better source of information than a broad web search. Assemble answers to these four key questions:

- *What are the known effects of the treatment?*

- *How is the intervention supposed to work?*

- *What could go wrong?*

- *What are the practical details?*

We'll guide you through each question.

Known effects. Ask what positive change you can expect to see in your child. This is where you consider the research evidence for the intervention. What data exists that indicates that this intervention helps children like yours? Ideally, you'd get a quick summary of published research for your answer, but for many potential interventions, such evidence does not exist. Again, this is not necessarily a bad thing, but it means that you need to make sure that all the other questions are addressed satisfactorily.

Dig into the effects in some detail. For example, consider persistence and carryover. What happens when the treatment stops? Do its therapeutic effects persist? What is the evidence for generalization and maintenance of an intervention?

Make sure to consider timing. How long would it be before you'd see this expected change? An excellent question to ask any therapist, doctor, or specialist is how you would know it's *not* working. What are the signs that the intervention is not effective, and when would be the right time to make this call?

Underlying mechanism. We're talking about cause and effect. The treatment, if it works as planned, should deliver specified effects caused by certain developments in your child that the intervention or treatment brings about. You want to know the plausible mechanism. For instance, you may ask a neurologist or psychopharmacologist how a proposed treatment changes brain function. The reason to ask is severalfold: it's an opportunity for you to learn from an expert, it serves as a basic check to assess whether the therapy (and possibly the therapist) makes any sense, and it sets the stage for you to be more of a partner with the provider. If, during your discussion, the expert uses too much professional language or jargon, don't be afraid to ask for a simpler explanation.

Side effects. If it hasn't already come up, find out about risks, side effects, and possible dangers of the treatment. One way to get at this is to ask what critics of this approach would say about its drawbacks and limitations. In some cases, consequences fall on others. Desensitizing a child who hates movie theaters by taking her to one may involve unpleasant outbursts that affect other moviegoers. Ask how to mitigate or monitor for risks and negative side effects.

The practical details. Try to understand the concrete aspects of the treatment or intervention. Ask specialists what they would actually do with your child. This will give you a sense of the time, location, sequence of steps, and other aspects of your child's experience and your own logistics. If you can't interview a provider, you may be able to find resources (for example, training materials) that provide practical descriptions of treatment steps in the library or online.

Understand the specifics entailed in the overall program of treatment: costs, tests, training and oversight for your family or caregivers, repeat visits to the doctor, or regular trips to a clinic. Don't forget to factor in transportation costs and logistical hassles. Some requirements affect practical or financial feasibility, and others may shift your assessment of how motivating or unpleasant the experience would be for your child.

Check That It Works for Your Child and Family

The final step is to decide whether the treatment will work in practice for your child and family. As a result of all your research, you now have a better understanding of your child's issues and treatment options. The preferred options may be clearer—and may include doing nothing for now. Your narrowly defined initial problem statement may now include wider goals, and your specialists may have helped you see how the approach they advocate can address multiple problems and needs, now and in the future. This is all good: you've learned more, and your approach is less piecemeal. At the same time, be sure to keep an eye on some specifics.

Practical Note:
Check That It Could Work in Practice

These four related questions can serve as a final check for your decision-making process:

- *Do the benefits outweigh the costs?*

- *Can it be customized for our needs?*

- *Are there interactions with other things we are doing?*

- *How will we keep an eye on effects?*

Use these questions to select interventions and treatments. We highlight the steps that can help you choose the best options for your child and family.

Benefits and costs. Take another look at feasibility, efficacy, and risks, based on everything you have just learned. Consider what your family may have to give up in order to make it work, based on costs, time, and effort. Your family is an interconnected system, and all of its members matter.

Customization. To ensure that the proposed treatment is a good fit, ask how it can be changed to mesh with your child's needs and other program elements, if necessary. Would such changes affect outcomes?

Interactions. Consider how this intervention relates to everything else in your child's program. This is important therapeutically. Talk it over with your team; some treatments may fit nicely with ones already in use, whereas others may not. Tell everyone who needs to know about supplements or other treatments you are already using that could interact with new treatments. Consider the overall approach: how consistent is the new treatment with other elements of your child's program? If it is consistent, probe whether it's needed; could it be redundant? If it differs from everything else you are doing, will you end up working at cross-purposes? If you must drop something to make room for the new intervention, is the trade-off wise?

Agree on a plan to monitor. Once you've decided to try it out, devise a specific plan for assessing the intervention's effectiveness. Specify what you expect to see. It's often valuable to have baseline data, which you collect ahead of starting a new treatment, as a basis for judging treatment effects. Work with the specialist and your team to devise a practical plan (timing, data collection strategy, review process) to establish as quickly as possible whether the intervention is working as anticipated. Make sure you all agree on the criteria for discontinuing and that you know the warning signs for negative effects that may arise.

You're now ready to take a closer look at the interventions, therapies, and treatments that are most likely to be on your list of options.

CHAPTER 8

Medications

As you consider every therapy option, it will be useful for you to know about the types of medications that may be suggested for your child. Despite tremendous growth in the understanding of and research into treatments, nobody can predict what will work for your child. Building on the framework designed to guide your assessment of each option, we'll discuss medications you are likely to encounter.

Medications will not be your child's only treatment, but they may play an important role as one element of your child's overall treatment. It is important to know what medications can and cannot do.

Approved Drugs for Autism

The US Food and Drug Administration (FDA) is the federal agency that reviews a potential new drug to decide whether to approve its use for the public. The FDA provides quality control through its careful screening of the evidence about how well each drug works. It also monitors side effects. Through the FDA and other professional agencies, doctors keep up to date with the status of drugs, so you'll be relying on the judgment and experience of your child's physician to guide you on the use of medication.

The drugs mentioned in this chapter have received FDA approval. No medication has yet been approved for the treatment of autism, meaning that there is no drug that addresses all the symptoms of ASDs. Some medications have been approved for treating specific symptoms related to autism.

Off-Label Uses

Some medications are used "off-label" to target particular symptoms. The term *off-label* means that a doctor uses a drug approved for one condition to treat symptoms of another condition, even if the drug has not been approved for the other condition. So, for instance, the drug gabapentin is approved for treatment of seizures yet is used off-label for other conditions, like bipolar disorder, pain syndromes, and restless leg syndrome, even though it has not been approved for these conditions.

It is a common practice in psychiatry to prescribe drugs off-label for children and adolescents. This is because although many of these drugs have not been tested in younger people, they have been found to have useful effects in adults. Clinicians who prescribe off-label to treat specific symptoms are considered to be practicing within medical standards. Off-label usage is neither illegal nor unethical.

Practical Note:
Always Check with the Doctor

As you consider a potential medication, be sure to work through your questions with your child's doctor, using the practical notes in the "Make Your Choice" section in chapter 7 as a guide. Your child's doctor can tell you whether a drug is approved. You'll also want to talk about off-label use. Don't be afraid to ask the doctor to clarify the reasoning behind the choice of medication. After starting a new medication, you may have new questions or doubts about the drug and its effects. Your child's doctor is there to answer these questions. It is important to note that if a medication will be stopped, it should not be done quickly and should always involve a doctor's oversight.

Before we move on to a more detailed look at specific drugs, we think it's a good idea for you to know about the kinds of studies used to evaluate medications.

How Drugs Are Studied

A medication or treatment cannot be said to be proven effective unless it has been examined in properly designed research with a large enough number of participants. In this section we'll look at the types of studies you are likely to read or hear about and consider key aspects of their design.

Types of Studies

There are many different ways to study whether a drug works. Let's review three common approaches.

Double-blind, placebo-controlled study. The most reliable type of study is known as a double-blind, placebo-controlled study. In this type of study, participants are randomly divided into two groups. One group of people receives the actual drug being tested. The other group receives a sugar pill (or placebo) that has been packaged to look like the real drug. Both drugs are labeled with an identifying code. Neither participants nor researchers know who gets the real drug and who gets the placebo. Because both participants and researchers are "blind" to who is taking what drug, the study is referred to as double-blind. This type of study reduces bias and limits the power of suggestion. People taking a placebo often report benefit, but if the people taking the real drug show significantly better outcomes, it strongly indicates that the drug works.

Open-label study. An open-label study is one in which both the person taking the drug and the researchers know what treatment is being administered. One problem with this type of study is that there is the power of suggestion, and expectation can significantly influence the outcome of research. Such studies can be helpful when two drugs are similar in action or when different doses of the same drug are being compared.

Crossover study. These studies are generally done on people with long-term conditions. In this type of study, participants are divided into two groups. Each group gets either the study drug or the placebo. At some point the groups switch: those taking the placebo are given the study drug and vice versa. A crossover study has the advantage that any variation between participants is reduced, because each participant crossing over serves as his own comparison.

Study Factors

Within studies are factors that can help you figure out how significant the information is. Here, we'll look at these factors.

Sample size. The sample size of a study is the total number of participants. The effects of a drug can be hard to measure with small sample sizes, which is why we regard studies that did not involve a large number of participants with caution. Although larger studies generate greater effects, they tend to include scant information on the particulars of each subject in the sample. Without details on study participants' characteristics, treatment histories, and experiences, it can be difficult to establish if the results apply appropriately to the individual case at hand. Nevertheless, because larger sample sizes make for statistically sound results, they are often the next step once small studies show promise.

Duration. The duration of a study is the length of time that a medication was tested. This is important because if a medication was not given enough time to work, positive results or negative side effects may have been missed. Also, the longer a drug is studied, the more we learn about its long-term consequences and benefits.

Replication. Replication is repeating the experiment and obtaining similar results. If a study uses the same drug as in an earlier study but finds different results, this means that the second study did not replicate the first. This may not be a reason to rule out a drug, but it could affect your decision about when and for how long to try it. Doctors tend to consider a drug more reliable when the results of studies have been replicated.

Why Consider Medications for Autism?

Although there is no medication cure, doctors prescribe medications for people with autism for several reasons. The overriding question is, will the child's life be better? If a medication is of value, the answer should be yes. Medications can help with five broad categories of challenges that affect children with autism:

- Inattention and hyperactivity

- Repetitive and stereotypical behavior

- Self-injurious behavior, aggression, and irritability

- Social impairment

- Co-occurring psychiatric, neurological, and other medical disorders

In the next section, we discuss how medications can tackle these challenges, but first, let's check the definitions of some terms just mentioned. *Stereotypical behavior* refers to repetitive actions whose purpose is not obvious to others. *Self-injurious behavior* can include head banging, hand biting, and other actions that damage the person's body.

Types of Medications for Autism Symptoms

There are thousands of drugs available, and new ones come to market all the time. To aid you in your navigation, we'll give you a quick guide to broad categories of the types of drugs that you may encounter, mentioning some specifics where we think it helps to clarify ideas. We'll use the categories of autism challenges outlined in the previous section.

Inattention and Hyperactivity

Inattention and hyperactivity commonly cause significant impairment in children with ASDs. Inattention reduces a child's ability to learn and benefit from other therapies and education services. Inattention may look different in a kid with an ASD when compared one who is diagnosed with ADHD alone, but the medications tried are often the same. The following classes of drugs target inattention.

Psychostimulants

Psychostimulants are commonly used to treat inattention and hyperactivity in ADHD, but studies have shown they have little, if any, effect on inattention in kids with autism. To make matters worse, side effects can include agitation, irritability, and even social withdrawal at higher doses. In the largest-ever trial of psychostimulants in children with ASDs (RUPP Autism Network 2005), seventy-two children between ages five and fourteen were given either the stimulant methylphenidate or a placebo. The results were that 49 percent of the children were considered to have benefited from methylphenidate and 18 percent had to discontinue the medication because of side effects (mainly irritability). Any improvement tended to be seen at lower doses, and hyperactivity and impulsivity improved more than inattention did. In typically developing kids, 70 percent of those with ADHD, but not with autism, respond to methylphenidate, with fewer than 2 percent stopping the drug because of side effects. For kids with ASDs, however, methylphenidate has more side effects and does not appear to help as much.

Nonstimulants

Atomoxetine. This drug is known as a selective norepinephrine reuptake inhibitor (SNRI) and is used to treat ADHD in children. In a double-blind, placebo-controlled crossover study of sixteen children with various ASDs, atomoxetine was associated with reduced hyperactivity (Arnold et al. 2006). Although this study was small in terms of numbers of children studied, results of this type generally lead to bigger trials.

Alpha-2 adrenergic agonists. The alpha-2 adrenergic agonists include clonidine and guanfacine. These drugs were developed to treat hypertension; they work by blocking the effects of adrenaline. Too much adrenaline acting on the brain can lead to agitation and hyperactivity. In a small study of eight children with autism, clonidine led to a reduction in hyperactivity, irritability, and stereotypical and oppositional behaviors as rated by parents, but clinicians did not observe the same improvements (Jaselskis et al. 1992). You, too, could encounter a situation where you find a medication to be helpful but your child's doctor does not see the improvements. Consider advocating for continuing the drug.

Children taking guanfacine, a longer-acting form of clonidine, showed less hyperactivity, less inattention, and fewer tics, with sedation being the most common side effect in one study of eighty children (Posey et al. 2004). Another study (Scahill et al. 2006) replicated these findings, noting that irritability and sedation were significant side effects. Because the results were replicated, you can give them more weight.

Repetitive and Stereotypical Behavior

Repetitive behaviors are considered central to ASDs, and they often interfere with social interactions. You will hear about *selective serotonin reuptake inhibitors (SSRIs)*, drugs that increase the amount of the neurotransmitter serotonin in the brain. Because they have been shown to be effective at reducing repetitive behavior in people with OCD, SSRIs have been considered for repetitive behaviors in autism.

Drugs That Increase Serotonin in the Brain

Many drugs increase the amount of serotonin in the brain. We'll review a few here, discussing insights that could apply to other choices.

Clomipramine. In a double-blind study of twenty-eight children with autism, clomipramine was found to be better than a placebo at reducing anger, hyperactivity, and obsessive-compulsive symptoms (Gordon et al. 1993). One major concern with clomipramine is that it can affect heart rate, so regular heart monitoring is essential. It is important to consider that some potentially helpful drugs may have serious side effects.

Fluvoxamine. Fluvoxamine has been found to be helpful in adults with autism; however, the results in children have been mixed. In one double-blind study of thirty-four children, there was no improvement in target symptoms when fluvoxamine was compared with a placebo (McDougle, Kresch, and Posey 2000). Here we see that a drug found to be helpful in adults is not necessarily helpful in children.

Fluoxetine. Fluoxetine is one of the most studied drugs in psychiatry and is used extensively in children and adolescents. In one study of thirty-nine children with ASDs, there was no reported difference between fluoxetine and the placebo (Hollander et al. 2005); however, in a smaller study, three of six patients showed a reduction in repetitive behavior and anxiety (Buchsbaum et al. 2001). Here, different studies give different results, but remember that no study will predict what the result will be in your child.

Self-Injurious Behavior, Aggression, and Irritability

Although many of the symptoms of autism can cause you and your child distress, perhaps nothing is more alarming than self-injurious behaviors. Antipsychotic drugs are most commonly used in this case, because while originally developed to treat schizophrenia, they are used in other conditions for their potentially powerful calming effect.

Antipsychotics

Haloperidol. One of the oldest antipsychotics, haloperidol has been studied extensively in children with autism. Various studies, such as one by Lowell Anderson and colleagues (1989), show that haloperidol at low doses helps reduce aggression, irritability, social withdrawal, and hyperactivity, with sedation and difficulty controlling body movement being the most common side effects. Unfortunately, difficulty controlling body movement can be so debilitating that haloperidol is rarely prescribed as a first choice.

Risperidone. Like haloperidol, risperidone has been extensively studied in autism. In studies reported in 2002, James McCracken and his colleagues

(RUPP Autism Network 2002) observed that risperidone showed such benefit for treating irritability, aggression, anxiety, depression, and repetitive behaviors that in 2006, the FDA approved its use for these symptoms in children and adolescents with autism.

Aripiprazole. In 2009, the FDA approved the antipsychotic drug aripiprazole to treat irritability, aggression toward others, deliberate self-harm, temper tantrums, and quickly changing moods in children with autism. An open-label study of 333 children with autism (Marcus et al. 2011) found that aripiprazole significantly reduced irritability and was generally safe and well tolerated.

There are many individual drugs within the antipsychotics class of medications, so if one antipsychotic does not show clear benefit or shows troubling side effects, it's well worth trying another drug in the class; however, other than risperidone and haloperidol, there is not substantial evidence that the benefits of these drugs outweigh the risks.

These drugs can cause serious side effects, which we'll discuss separately later in this chapter.

Social Impairment

Social and communication difficulties are universally found in ASDs. No drug has been found that makes it easier for a child to make better eye contact, communicate more effectively, or play collaboratively with her peers. But certainly, if your child is inattentive or irritable, attempts at socializing and communicating will be even more difficult. All of the drugs already mentioned, in particular risperidone, target some aspect of behaviors that can hamper socializing and communicating.

Co-occurring Psychiatric, Neurological, and Other Medical Disorders

Autism rarely occurs by itself; one or more co-occurring psychiatric disorders can emerge. Up to 80 percent of children with

ASDs experience intense anxiety symptoms (Leyfer et al. 2006). Anxiety disorders, such as OCD, social anxiety, and generalized anxiety disorder, and mood disorders, like depression, commonly accompany autism. Other treatable neurological conditions associated with autism include seizure disorders, ADHD, and Tourette syndrome. Also, it's important to recognize that children with autism may have other medical conditions that require medication management, such as asthma or diabetes. Medications for *any* condition can interact with the drugs we have reviewed in this section, so remember to mention all medications to your child's doctor.

Any co-occurring disorder can lead to a gradual or sudden worsening of behavior, so take a systematic approach to tackling behaviors and symptoms. Although we will not review medications for every general medical condition, we'll survey the types of drugs used for psychiatric and neurological symptoms, because you are more likely to encounter them.

Always consider medical problems when a child with autism develops new or more severe behavior problems. Pain and physical discomfort are often expressed as irritability, aggression, or self-injurious behavior (a child may hit the part of the body that is painful). There is nothing about autism that precludes ear infections, strep throat, or other medical issues. In fact, some gastrointestinal problems, like constipation, are more common in autism. Dr. Margaret Bauman, pediatric neurologist at Massachusetts General Hospital, transformed the way pediatricians think about this. Now they are more likely to consider possible medical causes of troubling behaviors in children with autism.

Antidepressants

Antidepressants like the SSRIs mentioned previously are used to treat depression and anxiety. However, research on their use in children and adolescents has led the FDA to warn doctors to use caution when prescribing them, because teens appear to be at risk for developing irritability and suicidal thoughts. It is not clear whether suicidal thinking occurs in children with autism. If you notice increased irritability or other behavioral changes in your child after starting antidepressants, talk to the prescribing doctor right away.

Mood Stabilizers

This class of drugs has been approved to even out mood swings in mood disorders such as bipolar disorder and to decrease seizures in disorders such as epilepsy. Mood stabilizers may be prescribed for a child with autism who has wide mood swings or excessive irritability.

Side Effects and Multiple Medications

Ancient wisdom reminds us, "One man's meat is another man's poison." Sometimes medications work well for the target symptoms in one person, only to cause side effects in someone else. Also, if your child is taking other medications, they may affect his response to a given drug.

Side Effects

Side effects range from a tolerable nuisance to extremely serious. Sometimes doctors use one medication to treat the side effects of another. This can even lead to side effects from both medications! Parents, doctors, and kids can find this whole process frustrating.

When you discover that your child is experiencing side effects, your child's doctor will advise continuing the medication and carefully monitoring it, reducing the dosage, adding another medication to treat the side effect, or stopping it altogether.

When it comes to side effects, some types of medications are particularly worrisome. As previously mentioned, antipsychotics include haloperidol and risperidone. Along with their benefits, these can cause high blood sugar, high fat content in the blood, and diabetes. They can lead to excess weight gain, which, in and of itself, is a serious medical condition that can increase the risk of developing diabetes. Another serious side effect is *tardive dyskinesia* (TD). Although rare, TD is a sometimes permanent condition that includes uncontrollable movements of the face, tongue, and other parts of the body. The risk of developing TD and the chance that it will become permanent are thought to increase with the length of therapy and the overall dose the child takes. Doctors who prescribe these drugs are very aware of this side effect and check for it during visits. Although very rare, *neuroleptic malignant syndrome* is a potentially fatal side effect of this class of drugs, particularly drugs like haloperidol. The signs and symptoms include high fevers; stiff muscles; shaking; confusion; sweating; changes in pulse, heart rate, or blood pressure; and muscle pain and weakness.

Multiple Medications

Using multiple medications is known as *polypharmacy*. Up to 20 percent of children between the ages of three and twelve years are prescribed four or more medications (Elder et al. 2009). It's important to know this as you consider research, because the majority of studies test only one medication at a time! Rarely are drugs tested in combination, and rarely are their interactions considered, so when your child's doctor recommends yet another drug, ask how it will interact with the drugs your child is already taking.

Navigating Medication Decisions

Medication can lessen the impact of the autism symptoms that most limit your child's ability to learn and participate in life. Drugs can help treat co-occurring disorders. As you've already heard, no sudy will predict what a given medication will do for *your* child. No medication is a cure-all, and all medications have potential side effects. Work closely with your child's doctor to assess whether the benefits of the medication outweigh its side effects. As the parent of a child who might have difficulty articulating her experience, you may need to be a detective as well as a collaborator. We hope that our guide to medications equips you for these important roles.

CHAPTER 9

Other Biomedical, Physical, and Sensory Interventions

Parents of children with autism often add vitamins and other supplements to prescribed medications as part of the overall treatment. But are supplements appropriate for autism? In this chapter we look at treatments that lie beyond those administered by mainstream medical professionals. We'll use the term *biomedical intervention* to refer to these supplements and physical and sensory treatments, noting that they range from well accepted to unconventional. The use of the term "biomedical intervention" for such treatments is common in the autism community (Rudy 2009). Here, we include sensory, occupational, and physical therapies, along with dietary and other treatments that fall outside the list of conventional medical treatments mentioned in the previous chapter. Other interventions change the environment, teach, or otherwise shape your child's interactions with others to target educational, social, language, expressive, creative, and practical goals; these are addressed in chapters 10 and 11.

The present review is in no way comprehensive. Research Autism (2011), a UK charity dedicated to research into interventions in autism, lists more than eight hundred autism interventions on its website! You can find research on electroconvulsive therapy, dolphin therapy, and massage, along with drugs and supplements from Abilify (aripiprazole) to zinc. Going through each item would require a separate book, so here, we look at some treatments you're most likely to encounter. If you find something promising, use the practice notes in the "Make Your Choice" section of chapter 7 to guide your exploration. We divide biomedical interventions into three broad categories: sensory interventions and exercise, dietary interventions, and biomedical therapies.

Sensory Interventions

Sensory interventions are therapy interventions that work on the five senses, the joints, and the muscles—in other words, the physical body—to benefit a person with autism. Some examples of sensory interventions are occupational therapy, including sensory integration; physical therapy; exercise; and auditory integration training, including the Tomatis method.

Occupational Therapy

Occupational therapists have a practical goal: to "help people across the life span participate in the things they want and need to do through the therapeutic use of everyday activities" (aota.org/featured/area6/index.asp). For people with autism, occupational therapy (OT) improves skills of daily living: toilet training, dressing, and grooming, for example. OT also addresses fine motor skills (such as holding a pen to write or using scissors to cut), gross motor skills (such as riding a bicycle or kicking a ball), perceptual skills (needed for managing your body in space and maintaining posture, as well as for distinguishing between shapes and estimating distances), visual skills (for reading and writing), and play skills. Therapists use activities like swinging to help kids process incoming sensory information and improve perceptual skills.

The work of an occupational therapist often overlaps with that of other team members. The scope of the therapy is broad and, as we've just seen, can include a wide range of activities. We will look at one component of OT that is sometimes also found as a separate therapy: sensory integration.

Sensory Integration

Our brains constantly receive inputs from the environment, which we perceive through smell, sight, sound, taste, and touch. Sensory information is useful only when combined by the brain; this yields a picture of the world around us that serves as the basis for our actions and responses. This ability to connect and calibrate information from the senses is called *sensory integration.*

Children with autism tend to respond to sensory information in ways that aren't typical, showing either overresponsiveness or underresponsiveness. The same child may underrespond to some sensory inputs and overrespond to others. When a person with autism receives a sensory message, his body and brain can have great difficulty integrating that information. His behavior might then not appear to match the nature and intensity of the sensation. Imagine a world where the sound of a distant lawn mower drives you crazy, the smell of someone's cologne makes you nauseous, or the caress of another's touch is so painful that you withdraw, screaming in agony. By helping to reset how senses are experienced, sensory interventions calm or change the experience of and behavioral responses to sensations that the person would otherwise find overwhelming (Ostovar 2010).

Physical Therapy

Physical therapists work on muscle development, strength, and coordination, targeting basic gross motor skills in young children, like sitting, rolling, and standing. As the child develops, physical therapists move on to help with skills requiring more complex coordination, such as kicking, throwing and catching, and skipping. The focus is more than just physical development, including the capacity for social engagement in sports and general play. The goals and approach of physical therapy can overlap with those of occupational therapy.

Exercise

The role of exercise in well-being is well established, and it might seem obvious to say that children with autism benefit from exercise. Some studies show that after moderate aerobic activity, children with autism experience increased attention span and correct responses to situations, as well as improvement in on-task behavior (Rosenthal-Malek and Mitchell 1997). Exercise can decrease stereotypical behaviors, aggression, and off-task behavior (Lang et al. 2010). Luckily, there are no reports of significant problems or side effects from exercise. In fact, exercise is considered so important that it is built into some educational programs. For example, vigorous physical exercise, emotional stability, and intellectual stimulation are the three cornerstones of the Higashi educational system. Of course, exercise is also a way to let out excess energy; develop mastery over physical tasks; train large and small muscle groups; and build strength, endurance, coordination, balance, flexibility, and body awareness—all of which address challenges faced by children with autism.

Auditory Integration Training and the Tomatis Method

Auditory integration training (AIT) stems from the theory that problems in hearing and processing auditory information can lead to behavioral or learning difficulties and that this is particularly true in children with autism. The idea is that if a child is very sensitive to certain sound frequencies, hearing those frequencies will be so intolerable that the sounds will lead to disruptive behavior, making it difficult for her to learn. During AIT, music *without* those frequencies is played to the child in two half-hour sessions every day for ten days. One specific form of AIT, the Tomatis method, requires the child to have AIT for 150 to 200 hours over the course of a year.

By exposing the child to only the sound frequencies that she can tolerate, the thinking goes, muscles that control hearing will be strengthened, eventually allowing the child to better tolerate previously unbearable sounds.

AIT proponents claim that the method leads to improved attention, expressive language, and auditory comprehension and processing, as well as decreased irritability and reduced lethargy. As with all of our other reviewed treatments, some parents swear by it. However, studies are inconclusive. AIT is not completely benign, and in some cases, severe behavioral problems and volatile mood swings have developed during treatment.

Dietary Interventions

About one in three children referred for evaluation for an ASD is started on a dietary intervention by the parents even *before* confirmation of diagnosis. One theory of autism is that certain foods cause allergies and that the allergic reaction interferes with the capacity to think. Another theory is that food allergies lead to bowel problems such as diarrhea, constipation, and vomiting, which result in poor nutrition. Others have suggested that it is not allergies but the foods themselves that are toxic to people with autism and that this toxicity leads to problems in thinking, learning, and processing of information.

Prescribed diets seek to eliminate certain food products (elimination diets) or add supplements that are considered to be missing. The following diets have been researched.

Gluten-Free, Casein-Free Diets

The gluten-free, casein-free (GFCF) diet is typically used for people with celiac disease or known sensitivity to gluten or casein. It is a diet that eliminates all dairy products and anything containing wheat, barley, oats, or other grains with gluten. Eliminating these items from the diet should prevent allergic responses in the gut and brain.

There have been one-off reports of dramatic improvements for people with autism who followed the diet religiously, but others have not benefited. A comprehensive review of the research failed to show that the GFCF diet helped people with autism. Further, an important concern is that the lack of dairy products affects bone growth. One study (Hediger et al. 2008) found that starting around ages five to six, boys with autism had significantly thinner bones than typically developing boys. Boys following casein-free diets had nearly half the bone thickness of boys with minimally restricted or unrestricted diets.

Food Supplements

Another theory is that children with autism need vitamins and minerals in doses higher than occur in the typical diet. Supplements usually include vitamins (A, B, C, D, E, and K) and minerals, such as calcium, magnesium, phosphorus, and zinc, as well as amino acids and fatty acids. The theory is that because people with autism appear to have difficulty with digestion, they don't absorb sufficient amounts of the vitamins and minerals necessary to deal with essential metabolic processes in the body and to maintain adequate brain function.

There have been many small studies on vitamin B_6, vitamin C, folate, magnesium, omega-3 fatty acids, and amino acids, as well as other supplements. Although there is little research indicating that supplements are of any specific help, they are considered safe. However, even if a supplement is safe, overdosing can occur. In particular, overuse of fat-soluble vitamins A, D, E, and K can be dangerous.

Biomedical Therapies

These therapies are borrowed from well-established use in other areas of medicine and are sometimes extended or changed for use in autism. For example, in standard clinical practice, chelation can treat acute poisoning, and antibiotics are used to treat bacterial infections.

Chelation

As an autism treatment, chelation is highly controversial: most mainstream medical professionals believe that the theory behind its use is flawed. *Chelation* involves giving a person certain chemicals, either by mouth or intravenously; the chemicals attach to heavy metals, such as mercury, and then are removed from the body.

The rationale for chelation as an autism treatment rests on the now-discredited idea that exposure to mercury and other toxic metals in the environment causes autism and that removing these metals from a child's body will improve her health. Despite no evidence that mercury or thimerosal causes autism, chelation has its advocates.

There are no controlled studies evaluating the safety or benefit of chelation, and there are severe dangers in administering chelating agents. In some cases chelation removes not only heavy metals, but also essential minerals like calcium, necessary for growth. Chelation can also lead to kidney failure, which has caused death in some children.

Secretin

Secretin is a hormone found in the human gut and involved in digestion. Of all the hormones, it is the one that has been most studied as a treatment for autism. No one is exactly clear how secretin might work for autism, but it was, for a time, considered promising after a single report that a child with autism who had been given the hormone showed dramatic improvement in eye contact and verbal communication. Extensive subsequent research reveals no evidence that secretin is effective as a treatment for ASDs (see, for example, Welch 2011).

Oxytocin

Oxytocin is a hormone that helps in childbirth and afterward by supporting the emotional connection between mother and child. It is sometimes called the "love hormone" or the "bonding hormone." Researchers believe that oxytocin plays a key role in enhancing social and emotional behavior and in regulating emotions.

Some studies show that people with autism have lower than normal levels of oxytocin in their blood. The thought is that if children with autism are given oxytocin, some of the associated social deficits will improve. One double-blind, placebo-controlled study (Guastella et al. 2010) used inhaled oxytocin in adolescents with ASDs. The adolescents then looked at photographs of people's faces. Those treated with oxytocin paid closer attention to the faces, spending more time looking at the eyes, which is an appropriate behavior. Because its side effects are few, given its potential benefits oxytocin is an intriguing option.

Hyperbaric Oxygen Therapy

Hyperbaric oxygen therapy (HBOT) is a method of giving pure oxygen so that the person receives ten to fifteen times more oxygen than if breathing under normal conditions. HBOT has been used as a treatment for people with traumatic brain injury and injuries caused by low oxygen states. One theory of autism is that there are fewer blood vessels in, and therefore less blood flowing to, the areas of the brain associated with autism symptoms. The idea of using oxygen is that high oxygen doses lead to the formation of new blood vessels in the brain and therefore improved brain function.

Small studies show some benefit with no side effects. A double-blind, placebo-controlled study of sixty-two children (Rossignol et al. 2009) found that children who received the treatment had "significant improvements in overall functioning, receptive language, social interaction, eye contact, and sensory/cognitive awareness compared to children who received slightly pressurized room air." This is another intriguing finding for future follow-up.

The Defeat Autism Now! Approach

Defeat Autism Now! (DAN!) is an approach that, according to protocol, can be prescribed only by DAN-certified clinicians. The approach uses an individualized combination of dietary interventions, vitamin supplementation, digestive enzymes, and even oral or intravenous chelation. The DAN! theory states that there are specific "biochemical irregularities" in each child who has autism and that by addressing these irregularities, autism can be treated.

Although there have been individual reports of remarkable outcomes, there are no well-designed studies. The approach is neither FDA approved nor accepted by mainstream clinicians. Further, chelation is highly controversial and potentially lethal.

Antibiotic and Antifungal Agents

Antibiotics and antifungals are drugs that are used in the treatment of various infections. Parents of children with autism report higher rates of respiratory and GI infections during the early years of the child's life. There have been reports of behavioral improvement in children with autism who are treated for these infections. One theory is that a poor bowel environment promotes the overgrowth of fungi and other microbes. Another theory is that the use of antibiotics for other infections kills off bowel bacteria, thereby allowing fungi to take over, and that the fungi produce chemicals that cause disordered thinking in children. Subsequently if the bowel fungi are killed, the child's thinking will become more organized and other autism symptoms will diminish.

There are stories of children who have had dramatic responses, but this does not bear out in large studies. Also, antifungal drugs are not without risk, and some can cause serious liver damage. Some children on antifungals get an upset stomach and become more hyperactive and irritable. Extensive antibiotic use has also led to the development of antibiotic resistance, meaning that future infections might not respond to the antibiotics and, as such, overwhelm the body's defense mechanisms.

Immune Therapies

Immune therapy involves administering antibodies to help a person fight off bacteria and viruses. One theory is that people with autism do not have a strong immune system and do not produce enough antibodies, which makes them more vulnerable to the infections that can cause some autism symptoms. There is no evidence of the effectiveness of giving antibodies to someone with autism. Further, the treatment is very expensive.

Considering All of the Biomedical Options

Because they may not involve prescription drugs or appear to be as invasive as other medical treatments, biomedical interventions for autism can appear simple and benign. But the truth is that these interventions are *not* necessarily less risky. Some of the approaches we've discussed entail the possibility of serious side effects. Also, because the interventions may not be supervised by a licensed professional, parents choosing to use them may need to be be extra-vigilant observers, noting changes, effects (or lack of effects), and all possible side effects over time.

It's important to let your team know about all treatments you are trying, so that behavioral changes can be put into context and considered along with all treatment interventions, including the educational approaches that we discuss in the next chapter.

CHAPTER 10

Education

Throughout our lives, the knowledge, skills, and capabilities we gain from one experience help us learn something new from the next. Learning is self-reinforcing. This is why early childhood education is thought to be so important.

Instruction also matters: how children are taught influences how much they learn. For a child with autism, the stakes are high. Education can affect future prospects and may even shift a child's diagnosis.

Enabling learning is part of every parent's job. It begins way before formal schooling starts, when we dangle toys to encourage an infant to develop his grasp or pretend not to hear a preschooler who demands a cookie without saying "please." In numerous daily interactions, we shape our children. But for parents of children who are not developing typically, it's not always clear what to do. To support learning for a child whose skills and capabilities are uneven, you'll need a customized plan. This chapter aims to help.

With a broad overview of learning serving as our foundation, we describe several approaches to educating children with autism. Our goal is to provide you with baseline knowledge for investigating the options that are feasible for your child. As you narrow in on approaches for your child, to ensure that he benefits from every opportunity to learn, you'll need to work with your own educational team. We'll share some practical advice on that front too.

Learning

Before we talk about education, let's look at learning. We use our own simple framework to examine its main ingredients.

Your ability to learn depends on your existing capabilities, knowledge, and skills, along with your interest, motivation, and feelings in the moment, plus your capacity to pay attention and be engaged. Of course, the specific situation—the task, the setting, the feedback you get from others, or the environment—is also crucial. Broadly, there are two sets of factors: (a) everything that you, as a learner, bring to the learning experience and (b) all that the experience provides. The latter includes methods of teaching, topics, materials, and so on. When we talk about education, we tend to look at the second set of factors. But the learner is just as important to the equation. So, what does your child bring to a learning opportunity?

Capabilities for Learning

Your child's interests are ingredients for enabling her learning, but there are many others. Capabilities for learning that are critical for people with autism include language and social capabilities, knowledge about the world and themselves, and physical and neurological development.

Language. It's hard to imagine traditional classroom instruction without speech and writing. Beyond formal communication, think of the vast amount of information conveyed by a teacher's tone, gestures, and physical interactions. Every aspect of language is important for making sense of others, expressing yourself, and adapting appropriately to the situation.

Social skills and relationships. Social capabilities enable us to navigate interactions, to solve problems and negotiate for what we want, to derive meaning from shared experiences, and to understand others. Your child draws on these capabilities with both grown-ups and other kids in countless ways every day.

Knowledge about the world. Both academic knowledge and practical, everyday knowledge about the world are important. Let's not forget kid-level culture, norms and social rules, and general knowledge of how things work (such as what a birthday party means and what's supposed to happen at one). And for practical and academic performance, skills and procedural knowledge (how to do long division or pack for an overnight trip) are also important.

Self-knowledge. Children's understanding of themselves evolves over time, from noticing and identifying bodily sensations and feelings, to knowing what is soothing or stimulating, to managing their own bodies and actions in order to avoid problems and generate good experiences, all of which facilitate self-regulation. Over time, children can better forecast how they may feel in the future or in other situations, allowing them to manage their own experiences. A further component of self-knowledge is psychological: the learner's sense of his own skills and capabilities, which may affect his confidence.

Physical and neurological development. Think of what becomes possible when a child can hold a pencil, catch a ball, or pour chemicals during a science experiment. Motor skills, muscle tone and strength, the capacity to focus on some sensory inputs while ignoring others, and the functioning of the body in everything from eye movements to digestion make learning possible by shaping attention, participation, and action. If you're physically uncomfortable, it's tough to focus on your math lesson.

Your Child's Learning Capabilities

Taken together, the preceding elements form a simple framework for looking at learning capabilities in people with autism. Our list is just a starting point: other capabilities, such as learning strategies, executive function, causal and critical thinking, and mathematical reasoning, are also important.

Each of us has a different profile across the areas. If we're lucky, as we grow up, we figure out how to offset our weaknesses with our strengths. You can help your child learn by selecting an educational approach that meets her needs based on her profile. For instance, traditional classrooms rely more on language than visual methods, making learning difficult for someone with language delays. Assessing your child's profile can also help you prioritize the therapies and teaching programs that will boost her ability to learn by shoring up needed capabilities.

Practical Note:
Profiling Your Child's Learning Capabilities

When you consider the capabilities we just listed, what do you think limits or enables your child's learning at school and in the world? Assess her readiness to learn based on the following:

- Her language and social capabilities

- Her knowledge about the world and herself

- Her physical and neurological development

Check your thinking with your team and focus your efforts on tackling these constraints. Understanding your child's profile may also help you at home with nonacademic learning.

Parents ask whether people on the spectrum learn differently. Research hasn't yet settled on an answer, but it has generated some insights that may help you understand—and appreciate—more about your child.

Intelligence, Learning, and Autism

Published studies present a perplexing picture of learning in people with autism. A substantial proportion of people with autism perform better than average in certain areas. Self-taught skills (for example, early reading, also known as *hyperlexia*; realistic drawing; piano playing), self-directed learning in areas of interest (for example, history or baseball statistics), and unusual capabilities (such as mathematical abilities) are all evidence of learning. An enduring puzzle of autism is that strengths are combined with poor performance in other areas. Some experts used to say that people with autism were not educable. Luckily, these beliefs have changed, even if their origins are understandable.

Someone with autism may perform poorly on standard intelligence tests, which rely on language. Alternative tests, such as Raven's Progressive

Matrices, avoid this problem. On this test, apparently low-IQ people with autism fare much better (Dawson, Mottron, and Gernsbacher 2008). Work with your team to figure out the validity of standard tests for your child. You may not have access to alternatives such as the test mentioned here, but you can still advocate for an appropriate perspective of your child's needs and abilities if evaluations do not reflect his underlying capabilities and potential.

Remember the pioneering researchers Kanner and Asperger (chapter 1)? Both thought that focused interests and abilities could be the means for people with autism to participate in and contribute to society. But even today, unusual interests can be seen as weird, even disparaged as abnormal, instead of as potential assets that actually represent learning in people on the spectrum (Dawson et al. 2007).

What about the behaviors commonly encountered in ASDs? Echolalia, which is the repeating of stock phrases or things others have said, may be an adaptive approach to learning language, according to some researchers. And self-stimulatory behaviors may help a person with autism regulate his own sensory input, facilitating rather than hampering learning. It can be helpful to remind your team and yourself that unusual behaviors may enable participation, attention, and learning.

If characteristic autistic behaviors are a result of the need to regulate sensory inputs, such as sound and sight perceptions, then teaching social behaviors directly ("Look me in the eye") may be futile or worse, because looking and listening in socially conventional ways are inherently difficult for someone on the spectrum. No wonder it's tough to generalize social skills across settings!

Among other strengths, excellent memory and remarkable attention to detail are common in people with autism. Do people with autism learn differently? One type of learning happens when we associate things with each other. Think of taking a shower: if you get water that's too cold or too hot a couple of times, you learn to use the controls correctly without thinking about it too much. This form of learning may be at least as good in people with autism as in neurotypical people. Interestingly, some research suggests that people with autism may be better at passive and observational learning than others, calling into question the value of experiential and other forms of sensory-based learning. When it comes to attending to stimuli—what you pay attention to—contradictory studies mean that we don't know whether people on the spectrum are over- or underselective. Still other areas, like hyperlexia, remain poorly explained.

Investigations into the thought processes of people on the spectrum are uncovering characteristic ways of thinking. One cognitive style more likely to be found in people with autism is known as *hypersystemizing*. Here's a quick explanation: their finely tuned senses mean that people with autism pay attention to details. All that attention enables the discovery of certain kinds of patterns in relationships—called "if p, then q" rules—that can be used to organize information and solve specific kinds of problems (Baron-Cohen et al. 2009). This is known as *hypersystemizing cognition*, a way of thinking that may account for some of the talents observed in people on the spectrum.

Despite this strength in finding patterns, people with autism appear to have uneven capabilities when it comes to forming and using mental categories, particularly when they are more abstract and social in content. People with autism may not organize information by using concepts in ways that neurotypical people do. This finding fits what people with autism have said about how they learn and think. Even the most talented and accomplished adults with autism encounter difficulty with certain creative activities, like writing, for example, when generating fictional characters who interact with each other in socially realistic ways.

Questions remain about how people with autism learn. Despite the need for much more research, we need not understand everything about the brain to make progress in education. To that end, we profile the teaching approaches you are most likely to consider.

Educational Approaches

Options for educating your child generally fall into a few clusters. One set of approaches is behavioral in origin, as we'll explain. The second set takes a developmental and relationship-based perspective. Other approaches combine aspects of both with other elements. Specific social- and communication-oriented approaches are discussed in the next chapter. Interventions presented elsewhere in this book may be more effective, at least when it comes to supporting evidence, but are more narrowly focused. Here we include only approaches for which we could find entire schools specifically designed for children with autism. If a school is based on the approach, we reasoned that it was broad enough to serve as an educational philosophy. Learn about these options so that you can choose what you'll advocate for at your child's school and embed into interactions with your child in every setting, including at home.

Behavioral Approaches

Behavior analysis is used in a variety of domains to understand and shape human behavior. The goal is to examine what people do and under what conditions they do it. The focus is on just two things: the person's behavior and the environment. The latter includes everything present that could affect behavior: the setting, the task, and the materials, along with what others say and do.

Seen through a behavioral lens, teaching seeks change in behavior (such as what a child writes in response to a test) by changing the environment (such as giving the child direct instruction). Applied behavior analysis (ABA) is the behavioral approach you're likely to hear about first. When it comes to educating children with autism, ABA may be used as shorthand to refer to a variety of related approaches. The term may also be misused to refer to a single element of the approach (such as discrete trial training, a form of structured teaching). It's important to clarify what you are talking about when referring to ABA for your child's education. We'll start you off with some basic information here.

In general, ABA is used to teach new skills, increase desired behaviors, reduce interfering behaviors, and maintain and generalize these changes. Generalization is the increase in the range of settings and conditions in which the sought-after behaviors take place (or increase in conditions under which undesirable behaviors do not occur). Professionals, aides, babysitters, or family members may provide ABA, but any nonprofessional will need training and oversight is always required.

Practical Note:
What Makes It ABA?

ABA is a systematic, evidence-based way of teaching that is customized to each child and for each specific goal. To deliver an ABA intervention, you must:

1. Identify the actual behavior you want to increase or decrease (which may be called the response).

2. Plan how to support this behavior change (for example, what stimuli, or triggers, will be offered).

3. Test your plan by arranging the environment, as best you can, to generate the stimuli so that the child behaves or responds as desired.

4. Reinforce the desired behavior with a direct reward or something indirect that comes later.

5. Track and act on relevant performance data.

In general, a proper program involves the right design and intensity, including as much as eight hours of programming a day for a preschooler. Appropriately trained teachers or paraprofessionals are essential, and you need sufficient oversight. A supervisor should watch the program in action, consult the data, and meet with the teachers or paraprofessionals. A common requirement is one hour of supervision for every week of ABA therapy delivered to your child; research appropriate standards when negotiating for your child's program. The standard professional qualification in the field is BCBA (board-certified behavior analyst).

It's *not* ABA if you do not see a clear specification of the desired (or undesired) behavior, along with a link to reinforcement, and useful data showing what was done and how well it worked. It's also not ABA if nobody looks at the data: we've seen time and money wasted on programs where pages of results were carefully entered but not appropriately interpreted, resulting in missed opportunities.

Here's a quick word on punishment or "aversives": behavioral programs no longer use punishment (in the most extreme cases, an exception may be made for violent or self-injurious behavior). Instead, teachers simply do not reinforce. As in all professions, there is a code of practice for behavioralists (for example, at bacb.com).

ABA approaches can be used in highly structured ways at home or at school to teach very specific things. For instance, you can use ABA to teach a child the numbers one to ten—a relatively rote task. But you can also use ABA to help her learn which ones are bigger and which are smaller, and how symbols map to quantities, which is called number correspondence. This may take more work, but as long as you break the task down into small steps and teach each step systematically, you can make progress using this method.

ABA can also be used incidentally and for social interaction: if you would like your child to say "hi" to anyone who greets her, you may start with discrete trial training (while sitting at a table, the teacher says, "Hi," and the child is reinforced when she replies appropriately). Eventually, you move to everyday life, where you expect your child to say, "Hi," when a guest comes into your house. If you reinforce her (with a verbal congratulation, or even just a smile, or by rubbing her shoulder—whatever works), you are using an incidental approach that makes the most of circumstances.

Specific Behavioral Approaches

A variety of specific behavioral interventions are often part of an ABA program. Along with discrete trial training, the tool kit includes assessments. The *Assessment of Basic Language and Learning Skills* (ABLLS) measures deficiencies in language, academic, self-help, and motor skills. Results are used to design and monitor individualized interventions. *Functional behavior assessment* delves into the conditions and effects surrounding a given behavior from the child's point of view. It can address puzzles in generalization and problem behaviors. A systematic teaching approach called *verbal behavior* teaches functional language and may help your child develop basic frameworks for communication. There are hybrid approaches too. For instance, Pivotal Response Treatment pairs behavioral teaching with content and rewards that are most meaningful to the child (Koegel and Koegel 2006).

The Evidence for ABA and Its Applicability

ABA is the core of many, if not most, intensive early intervention programs for young children with autism. Of all educational approaches, it has the best evidence base (Vanderbilt Evidence-Based Practice Center 2011). This is not to say that it's the best option, just that it is the most researched. If you consider how ABA works, this makes sense, because each program collects a lot of data and methods are relatively standardized. As a result, the professional practice of ABA contributes to knowledge in the field as a whole.

ABA is thought to be most beneficial in specific uses for intensive early intervention for young children, addressing challenging behaviors and certain aspects of communication and social interaction. When it comes to ABA for more complex academics, evidence is weaker or nonexistent. In general, ABA can't be used to figure out what your goals should be and what's most important for your child to develop or learn next. And if the child encounters challenges due to sensory issues, a purely behavioral treatment may fall short (although an excellent functional behavior assessment may alert you to the need for a sensory assessment by revealing how behavior varies across environments).

The practice of ABA is evolving as new insights arise. Within the ABA community, growing interest in "positive behavioral support" emphasizes praise (rather than tangible rewards, such as edible treats), recognizing that interactions with cherished others trump rewards from neutral adults. Today's continuum of approaches to teaching children with autism includes promising blended approaches, such as Pivotal Response Treatment, mentioned previously. Another example comes from the Early Start Denver Model, which pairs developmental, relationship-based play intervention with ABA. Toddlers with an ASD diagnosis randomly assigned to this treatment made significant gains in language and everyday life behaviors compared with peers who were referred to commonly available programs and treatments. (Dawson et al. 2010). So, what are these developmental, relationship-based approaches?

Developmental Approaches

We look at two explicitly developmental perspectives: (a) the developmental, individual-difference, relationship-based approach and (b) relationship development intervention.

The Developmental, Individual-Difference, Relationship-Based (DIR) Approach

Child psychiatrist Stanley Greenspan and his colleagues developed the DIR framework and its application to interacting with and teaching children with autism (Greenspan and Wieder 2006). The *developmental* aspect draws on studies of child development that identify social, interactive, and cognitive capacities needed to:

- Pay attention appropriately

- Engage with and relate to others

- Initiate and respond to all kinds of communication

- Interact with others to solve problems together

- Use ideas to communicate, to think creatively, and to play imaginatively

- Connect concepts, derive insights, and tackle complexity and ambiguity

DIR methods are designed to help children develop these capacities.

The second key aspect of DIR is *individual differences*. Each child's biology and sensory profile is unique: sensory overreactions or underreactions, processing difficulties, and poor control of physical responses affect the child's ability to draw on and develop his capacities and must be taken into account to enable learning and participation.

The third aspect of DIR, *relationships*, highlights the importance of emotions. How a child feels in the moment determines how hard he works during an interaction, and relationships are the means for tapping into and influencing these feelings. Teachers and caregivers aim to use the child's feelings—positive or negative—as vehicles for building engagement, which ultimately advances emotional development.

At this point you may be thinking, *This is all good, but how do I help my child develop?* The starting point for DIR treatment, called Floortime, is a feedback loop of communication between the child and others. If children can be enticed and guided to engage in more, larger, and increasingly sophisticated circles of interaction, the thinking goes, they build capacities most needed for learning and development. Adults shape the child's learning by pushing for the next level of development in their interactions, adjusting their interactions as they assess the quality and quantity of communication circles. Every DIR interaction starts with engaging the child in his current state of skills, interests, and capabilities to bring him along toward the next stage of development. The object of the interaction is not as important as the developmental level and prospects for engagement it entails. So it may be worth talking about your child's intense interest for a few more months if it can help you draw him into more sophisticated interactions. The term "Floortime," by the way, comes from its use with young children, for whom DIR involves playing on the floor; for older children, floor play is a metaphor for engagement around their interests. To enable effective DIR interventions, the PLAY (Play and Language for Autistic Youngsters) program adds systematic parent training and structured home visits in which expert consultants provide modeling, coaching, and video feedback (Solomon et al. 2007).

With DIR, your aim is to help your child to move up the rungs on a developmental ladder, each of which must be mastered before moving to the next. As with any educational intervention, you start by assessing your child's current level of development and use the framework to establish a sequence of goals.

Social, language, motor, emotional and problem-solving aspects are intertwined in a customized DIR intervention, complicating the aggregation of results required for clinical research. Look for more studies to emerge in the coming years.

The skills of a play-based therapist are subtle, because the treatment can look just like really fun free-form play. DIR Floortime may appear on your service provider's menu of options, but as with behavioral programs, it's important to confirm that therapists are appropriately trained, supervised, and mentored (DIR certification is available). Even better, engage in the treatment yourself. Families can learn from books and other materials as well as workshops and consultants.

Relationship Development Intervention (RDI)

Developed by psychologist Steven Gutstein (2009) and his colleagues, RDI uses everyday interactions to advance emotional, social, and cognitive development. Parents develop their own skills and awareness to create appropriate opportunities for a child to solve new problems in the course of everyday life. The goal is to increase children's ability to respond to challenges thoughtfully, flexibly, and creatively while marshaling communication skills. Rather than evaluate only the child, RDI also assesses child-family relationships, because a goal of the therapy is to advance the relationship. Certification is available for RDI therapists.

RDI is built on the idea that exposure to the right types and sequence of challenges encourages children's brains to develop. Specific goals for treatment include building emotional referencing abilities (understanding others' emotional experiences); social coordination and collaboration; language skills for interaction; adaptable thinking, particularly in creative problem solving; and reflection and foresight skills.

A small amount of published research supports RDI, but as with other developmental interventions, it does not yet amount to evidence that the approach is superior to alternatives.

Other Educational Approaches

Other methods for teaching children with autism include some that have been around for decades, such as Daily Life Therapy, pioneered by the Higashi schools, and TEACCH (Treatment and Education of Autistic and Related Communication-Handicapped Children), the latter of which we'll describe briefly. The SCERTS Model, a more recent arrival, draws on a variety of approaches and therefore seems to be a fitting conclusion to this section.

TEACCH

Psychologist Eric Schopler and his colleagues at the University of North Carolina developed TEACCH as the basis for teaching in separate special-education classrooms within public schools. Some early evidence supported the approach, but little has appeared in recent years. The program's four decades of continuity and its use in hundreds of classrooms is the result of an ongoing collaboration among parents, researchers, and other professionals; the university; and the state of North Carolina.

Accommodation lies at the heart of TEACCH. Its classrooms have workstations with carefully laid-out instructions and materials, providing visual clarity to enable students to carry out their work and increase their receptiveness, understanding, organization, and independence. The TEACCH approach is encapsulated in "structured teaching," which entails:

- Understanding the culture of autism, "the characteristic and predictable patterns of behavior in individuals with this condition" (Mesibov, Shea, and Schopler 2004)

- Developing an individualized plan for each student, rather than using a standard curriculum

- Structuring the physical environment

- Using visual supports to make activities and tasks predictable and understandable

Several books present the TEACCH model, although they are written for teachers, not families. As with all other programs described here, resources are available online.

The SCERTS Model

Combining *social communication, emotional regulation,* and *transactional support,* the SCERTS Model is an assessment-based framework. Designed to be practical and integrative, it provides guidelines for advancing social communication and preventing problems that interfere with learning and the development of relationships. Parents, teachers, and therapists can use SCERTS to select priorities for treatment. It includes a family component.

A multidisciplinary team of experts drew on their professional experience and research evidence to define the three targets of SCERTS: independent and functional communication, managing emotions and stress, and accommodating needs while leveraging interests (Prizant et al. 2005). One strength is its applicability to a range of ages, developmental abilities, and settings, with assessments that are designed to be meaningful and customized to the family. Its framework may be used for ongoing monitoring to ensure quality and consistency. A downside is that it's difficult for parents to implement on their own, because the book-length documentation is fairly complex. SCERTS can incorporate practices from varied approaches, including Pivotal Response Treatment, TEACCH, DIR, and RDI.

Its grounding in research on child development sets SCERTS apart from traditional ABA approaches. And its goal, to support "authentic progress" (Prizant et al. 2007), emphasizes learning and independently using functional, appropriate skills with various partners and settings. That worthy goal seems to us as good a place as any to wrap up our survey of educational approaches for children with autism. May we all help our children make authentic progress!

Three Pieces of Advice for Choosing Educational Approaches

The combined approaches taken by SCERTS and the Denver model are being studied in use. Each is carefully based on established research. While it may seem like a great idea to pair two methods—the evidence and systematic nature of behavioral perspectives with attention to motivation, initiation, relationships, and developmental paths—this doesn't necessarily mean that an ad hoc combination of methods is good. If your school offers an eclectic approach, dig deeper. Ask the same type of questions we've suggested throughout this book: *What are the criteria for selection of each method? How will we know it's working?*

Look at every potential educational approach through the lens of what you know about your child's needs, strengths, and profile of learning capabilities. Use your team to help assess how well a given approach would match, drawing on the ideas from this chapter.

And at the end of the day, you may not have the flexibility to switch schools or allow your child to attend the school you'd like. It's likely, however, that you'll find aspects of some of the approaches we've discussed incorporated into a program within your child's current or prospective school. You may add extra therapies at home, some of which you and your family members facilitate, relying on books, workshops, or consultation for help in doing so. Even if you face limited choices, equipping yourself with some knowledge of the options will help you work with the school team and others to shape the plan that's best for your child. In the next section, we'll discuss this process.

Working with Your Educational Team

Today's educational methods for people with autism emerged from research that began in the middle of the last century, but the resulting teaching techniques and programs spread only in the past decade or two. Before 1975, the vast majority of children with ASDs did not get to learn in public schools. Many were placed in long-term institutional care with poor educational opportunities.

Why are things better today? Parents who advocate for their children have always been agents of change. We can also thank science and the medical and therapeutic professions for the spread of knowledge and the evolution of interventions, therapies, and teaching. Let's not forget lawyers and legislators. To get a sense of what has been enabled by all these efforts, let's look at the process likely to determine your child's programs and placement.

The Formal Educational Plan

Most parents of children with ASDs in the United States, Canada, and other developed countries work with the public education system to define a plan for their children. (Elsewhere, options are fewer, and to the extent that they can, parents find, manage, and pay for specialized education themselves. Although we focus on the United States, it may be useful to remember that not all families confronting autism have the same options.)

In the United States, the first option for tapping into the educational system for parents of children with autism is an *individualized education program* (IEP), the official blueprint for the academic year that defines how your child will be taught, supported, and accommodated to get the education she needs, whether in a regular-education public school or a full-time institution. For children under age three, the plan may be known as an individualized family service plan; for school-age children who require only accommodation, it may be called a "504 plan" (after the section of related law). We'll use the term "IEP" to refer to any written plan.

Your Family's Rights

Under US law, children must be educated in the "least restrictive environment." If the appropriate supports and accommodations enable your child to learn in a regular-education classroom, that's where she should be. Only if it's not possible for them to learn in regular-education settings should children be placed in separate classrooms or schools.

You are legally entitled to be involved in planning and monitoring your child's program. Parents and the school district are supposed to be partners; schools can't dictate the program (nor can you!). You have the right to reject a proposed plan, after which you work with the legal system to find a solution. For more information, consult a book like Lawrence Siegel's *The Complete IEP Guide* (2011), one of several very useful resources for parents embarking on the process.

Current law supports teaching students with disabilities using instructional approaches that are consistent with what is known scientifically to be effective. It's linked to a key theme in the law: the notion of appropriateness. Your child is entitled not to the *best* education, only to a free and *appropriate* public education that meets her needs. This, of course, means that you have to sort out what you think is appropriate and convince the school district that you're right. For some parents, this can involve disappointment, because they, naturally, want what's best for their child. If you end up in a dispute with the school system, defining what you seek as "appropriate" is part of the battle. This is why we suggest looking at the evidence for each approach under consideration.

Who Gets to Decide and When

When it comes to major decisions, the formal IEP team should include one or both parents; the child's teacher or prospective teacher; a representative of the local education agency authorized to provide or supervise special education; the child, if appropriate; and possibly other individuals chosen by the parents or the public agency. The team often includes specialists who provide therapies to your child (speech and language therapists, for example); you may also include an expert consultant, your child's doctor, or even an advocate to help you make the case for your child's needs.

Usually, an IEP meeting takes place annually, in advance of the new school year. Inputs include assessments and reports from service providers.

The team is supposed to start by discussing the child's profile in light of these inputs and then consider goals, programs, and placement. The meeting may necessitate preparation and planning, and it can cause stress for parents because much is at stake. Critical times include when your child is first diagnosed, whenever there is the possibility of a school change, and when planning for the transition to adulthood.

Formal team meetings may also be called when your child encounters difficulties at school that require reassessing his plan. Some teams hold routine update meetings midyear or more often.

Building and Managing Your Own Team

If you're like most parents we know, you want to be involved in your child's education beyond formal meetings. We suggest that you build your own informal team with those most closely involved in teaching and treating your child. This isn't your official IEP team but one that you will organize and manage. It needn't be anything too complicated.

Why Build an Informal Team?

There are many reasons to build your own team. Outside school, most children with autism benefit from treatment at home, in specialist sessions, and in the community. Your child may work with family members or volunteers, the school district's home program providers, and behavioral, social, or other therapists whom you hire privately. Music, art, or dance therapies could be in the mix. Given how difficult it is for children with autism to generalize what they are learning, consistency is key. Learning from and coordinating with everyone is clearly important. Without building some form of a team, this is very difficult to do across domains.

Parents who homeschool benefit from talking to others about overall approach, goals and measurement of progress, specific teaching methods, curriculum, materials, activities, websites, and other resources. And just having a sounding board is valuable.

Practical Note:
Goals for Your Own Educational Team

What will you accomplish with your team? Consider these options to select your top priorities.

- Ensure that teaching and therapy are aligned with the specifics of your child's profile.

- Coordinate so that you're all on the same page; this is especially key in behavioral challenges (phobias, self-injurious behaviors, aggression), as well as practical communication and daily life skills.

- Provide team members with a reason to review your child's performance, gather data, and generate reports or treatment notes.

- Monitor and assess new interventions; change course if needed and celebrate small wins.

- Provide context by sharing family background, school culture, and so on. Your child's relationships and social experiences are important for everyone to understand.

- Reprioritize objectives as needed. Plan for upcoming events, curricula, and opportunities.

- Tap into different people's expertise. Hold brainstorming sessions concerning tricky problems.

- Identify and tap into your child's emerging skills, interests, and capabilities.

- Add a new dimension of learning and collaboration across disciplines that is professionally rewarding for team members, increasing their engagement with your child and family.

Planning and Scheduling Your Meetings

Since this is your team, it's up to you to choose who's on it, taking into account what's feasible. The overlap with your IEP team may vary. You are likely to want to include your child's teacher.

Practical considerations are likely to determine what's possible. One mother touched base with her son's kindergarten classroom teacher for fifteen minutes every Friday, forming a strong two-person team. But this is the exception. In most cases, finding time to meet with school staff is difficult: educators are already stretched thin with too many students and not enough hours in the day. Your relationship with teachers will be smoother some years than others (as every parent of a school-going child knows!). You may need to improvise. Instead of fretting about not being able to meet with the classroom teacher, plan monthly check-ins with a home therapist, your spouse, and your child's speech and language therapist, using some of the methods outlined next to share meeting results with the classroom team. This is one reason to develop your own practices for communicating and collaborating with others, so that you can support everyone who works with your child year to year.

Your team may be just a couple of people who touch base regularly. You could even work with people you have never met: consultants can call in to advise you, and online communities for homeschooling offer extensive support. Can you use technology in creative ways? A virtual team can meet by phone or web conference. Some parents use a private blog or wiki to interact with team members on an ongoing basis, posting reports or questions to get others' input.

How often do you connect? Many teams meet quarterly, but others may meet every six weeks or monthly, depending on the situation. In general, if meetings are frequent, you'll likely focus on just a few items per meeting. Less frequent meetings may have longer agendas.

And if finding a time to meet is too difficult, there are options. One family sent a weekly e-mail update describing developments and events in their child's life, mentioning emerging interests and skills and upcoming opportunities. After school finished every June, they hosted a cookout, using the festive occasion to thank everyone and introduce people to each other. They encouraged team members to contact each other (note: due to the US law known as HIPAA, the Health Insurance Portability and

Accountability Act, you need to give therapists written permission to share information about your child).

Running an Effective Team Meeting

Don't underestimate the impact of setting agendas, managing time, and sending out quick follow-up notes to document team decisions and next steps. They are invaluable habits for managing a team.

Practical Note:
The Power of a Well-Run Meeting

Invest in making every meeting as effective as possible by taking the right steps before and after each meeting. If your team has only an hour, how do you use it wisely? Here are some suggested agenda items for which it's most useful to have an interactive team discussion:

- Tap into everyone's input to identify priorities, discussing what's most crucial.

- Focus on complex issues that cannot be sorted out by e-mail or phone and those for which it is most crucial that you get multiple points of view.

- Address action items: the most pressing current issues for which you can make a difference.

- Look beyond problems to include new opportunities enabled by your child's development.

- Counterbalance a reactive approach—responding to emerging issues and changes—with a more proactive approach informed by what your team sees as the most important next step for your child. What does your team seek for your child, based on knowledge of child development paths?

Practice the art of team building. Ahead of time, talk to people about what they want out of the meeting and then use their ideas to create a brief agenda. If you cannot cover everything suggested, list extras as additional items and next steps. Several days before you meet, send out your agenda and any reports or briefings from therapists and teachers that would be useful preparation, and have an extra copy or two on hand. During the meeting, emphasize specific decisions and next steps. End each segment of the meeting with a quick check, and do a review at the end: what will happen as a result of this discussion? Who's going to do it? When? Managing time carefully is key. If you have three agenda items, allocate 25 percent of your time to each, and reserve the remaining time for new items that may come up. End on time, making sure to say something that is appreciative and specific about the work of each person in the room.

Becoming Your Child's Best Advocate

We end with one more practical suggestion. Every idea, piece of information, and tip laid out in this chapter is designed to do one thing: enable you to help your child learn. The relationships you build with your educational team, your knowledge about IEPs and the law, and the specific educational approaches you push for—all are means to this end.

So, we think it's worth your time for you to write and share what you've learned. Develop your own picture of your child, how she learns, her strengths, and your vision for her. A video and other material could also be part of the package, but a written document should be the core. Update it at least once a year. Keep it short and focused, to two or three pages. You will use it again and again. It can serve as input to the IEP process. Share the document with teachers, therapists, and staff. Don't forget babysitters, camp counselors, and even your relatives.

Practical Note:
Developing a Useful Profile of Your Child

Call this document "How My Child Learns." We suggest structuring it as follows:

- Open with a short paragraph that mentions your child's name, age, and school and some family information. Add a sentence or two about her special interests. Mention things that teachers or therapists have told you they appreciate about her.

- Include a paragraph or two about your hopes for your child.

  Writing down these goals and dreams conveys to others what matters to you as a family; and when the day comes that one of your hopes actually materializes, you won't take it for granted! For years, one family listed "asking us questions" as a dream for their child with autism. As he developed, his skills grew, and one day the parents realized he had asked them a question. This particular development followed from others, so they may not even have noticed it. But realizing that this had been a hope of theirs for some five years made them appreciate it and celebrate it. It was a good moment on a difficult journey for everyone, and it gave the entire family hope for the child's future.

- Include a list of all the ways that your child learns. Base it on your own experience and what you learn from everyone who works with him.

  If you need a starting point, draw on the learning capabilities framework in this chapter to organize the ideas and check for completeness. For example, if your child is sensitive to sound, mention that he learns better in a quiet environment, in the presence of white noise, when wearing noise-canceling headphones, or when the teacher uses a microphone system that transmits to your child via an earpiece during classroom group instruction.

Working on such a list is a great way for you to make the most of the professionals and paraprofessionals around you to develop your understanding of your child. Ask for their help to refine the list every year. Get their feedback. Add to and edit this list as you go, whenever you discover something new. Back up the points with specific examples from your child's experience (for example, refer to a report by an occupational therapist or include a photograph of a classroom workstation layout that worked particularly well). As you learn more about research or as you talk to specialists, look for evidence that backs up what you know works for your child. Include useful specifics as you learn more about instructional methods, teaching approaches, and classroom accommodations.

For example, one mother learned about a concept called *reduction in task demand*, which refers to making work easier to do. She mentioned in her document that her teenage son benefited from being taught using this approach in his mainstream classroom. Because she had learned about the idea and mentioned it in writing, she could take her learning further. Talking with her child's team, she learned that tasks could be made less demanding via either of two strategies. The depth of assignments, material, and assessments could be modified (for instance, when his teacher rewrote his history test to make the questions easier, enabling him to take his test in class with his peers). In other cases, the teacher reduced the number of assignments but expected the child to complete the work to the same depth as peers (for instance, the boy wrote a report on only one geographical element, while each of his classmates reported on several). Each type of modification entailed *different* preparation and *different* implications for the child's participation and learning—simply cutting his history test short was easier to do than rewriting his test to make it easier to complete. What would benefit him most and be feasible for the teaching team? It was useful to discuss the question in their IEP meeting. The mother asked the team to consider setting aside teacher preparation time, as well as time for the teacher and her colleagues to review which tasks were being modified, how, and whether the student's learning needs were being served well by the chosen strategy for task demand reduction.

For every child, getting an excellent education is important. But for children with autism, an excellent education that misses the mark may be a tragedy. It's frustrating to learn that education is important and most likely to offer the best chance for improving your child's prospects, only to find that the exact methods and approaches for optimal teaching haven't been specified yet and probably never will because every child is unique. But you have many years to parent your child, and you have many chances to learn as you go and build on your knowledge of what works for your child. Your team, your own learning process, and, of course, your child's unique capabilities and interests are all key ingredients. We hope that the ideas in this chapter will help you make the most of them.

CHAPTER 11

Social, Communication, and Language Interventions

How can you help your child engage more meaningfully with the world? We'll take a look at interventions designed to address communication, language, and social interaction, focusing on specific therapies, treatments, and interventions you may consider. In autism, every aspect of the condition and its treatment seems to be interconnected, and that is particularly true when social interaction and communication are involved. So we won't draw too many distinctions among the domains; we will instead look at some specific interventions and describe each briefly, discussing key issues, such as implementation. Where it makes sense to do so, we'll mention how the evidence stacks up.

Speech and Language Therapy

Language skills vary widely in autism. Some people with autism do not speak. Others have spelling skills that are off the charts, teach themselves to read at age two or three, develop adultlike vocabularies in elementary school, or talk in great detail and at great length on topics of interest to them. But there are some common challenges. Many find it difficult to use language effectively, particularly in social interactions. Many speak with unusual rhythms and tones or overly formal language. It's common for people with autism to have a hard time deciphering the meaning of spoken and written language, body language, tone, and intonation and to struggle with responding appropriately.

Language includes speech, writing, symbols, and gestures, all seen through the lens of context and setting. For a child who has difficulty perceiving, processing, and integrating sensory information, the challenge is to make sense of how the nonverbal communication fits with the words. It's not helpful but a hindrance that communication in any social setting is multichannel, with gestures, expressions, and tone shaping the meaning of what is said.

Starting early helps. Enabling even young children to better interact with others can make a big difference over their lifetimes, because it supports subsequent learning and development. In speech and language interventions, this involves assessing and identifying the best way to improve communication and enhance the child's quality of life. With early identification and intervention, two out of three preschoolers with autism improve communication skills and their grasp of spoken language. Those who receive the most speech therapy tend to improve the most.

Speech therapists are likely to be part of your child's treatment team. These professionals are also known as speech-language pathologists (SLPs). A certified SLP holds at least a master's degree and is trained to treat a variety of speech and language problems. Some specialize in autism, so it's worth inquiring about the experience and special training of a prospective therapist.

One invaluable role of an SLP is to prioritize, design, and deliver therapies that address the most critical needs for the child's social communication, taking into account your family's specific constraints and what is important to you. These professionals should know of and draw on the current body of knowledge regarding effective approaches to meeting the specific needs of children with ASDs and their families. According to the professional organization for speech therapists (ASHA 2006), an SLP's goals include enabling your child to:

- Initiate spontaneous communication in functional, useful activities, with different social partners and across settings.

- Understand both verbal and nonverbal communication in social, academic, and community settings.

- Communicate reciprocally to help develop friendships and social networks.

- Use and understand both verbal and nonverbal means of communication, including natural gestures, speech, signs, pictures, and written words.

- Access literacy and academic instruction and curricular, extra-curricular, and vocational activities.

Part of an SLP's job is to help the team address communicative aspects of problem behaviors and support positive behavior. For instance, a speech therapist can help a child develop and use more functional alternatives to challenging behaviors. Sometimes called *functional communication training*, this approach aims to reduce undesired behaviors (Tiger, Hanley, and Bruzek 2008).

Other SLP tools and interventions include introducing alternatives to speech for children who are nonverbal or who would benefit from augmenting their spoken language. Speech alternatives include sign language, typing, and using picture boards with words. Communication technologies for supporting people with autism include "electronic talkers," which generate speech based on the person's physical input. These devices cater to a wide range of abilities: some use pictures or icons for input, while others rely on keyboard typing. The output is spoken words. Portable devices can be attached to a laptop, car seat, or wheelchair.

Not all speech and language–related therapy is provided by an SLP. Everyone who interacts with your child uses language with her, after all! And the work that other therapists and teachers do with your child may be closely connected to your SLP's work. For instance, a therapist providing Pivotal Response Treatment may employ reciprocal imitation training to teach nonverbal behavior by imitation. Verbal behavior, often part of an ABA program, entails direct teaching of language.

Families are essential in this area. Even if all you have is a book, you can learn useful techniques to support speech and language development; an excellent parent-friendly example for younger children is The Hanen Centre program (Sussman 1999). Family training by specialists is part of many developmentally oriented programs, as we described in the last chapter.

The traditional approach to speech and language treatment in schools, via relatively infrequent pullout sessions, is not as effective as more intensive, integrated approaches. So to support your child's development and learning, your speech therapist must connect with the rest of your team to share insights, learning, strategies, techniques, and supports. If at all possible, your SLPs should overlap with others who work closely with your child.

What Do Speech Therapists Actually Do?

The nature of an SLP session depends on the child. Your toddler's speech therapist may come to your home, but for older children, therapy sessions take place at school or in the therapist's office. In schools there may be a mix of one-on-one pullout sessions, classroom activities, and small group sessions. There are also consultations between the speech therapist and teachers. The therapist will use games, toys, books, and all kinds of fun activities to draw your child in and extend the interaction. The SLP could be so good that if you didn't know the session was therapeutic, you might think that it was just an excellent playdate!

Speech therapists work on different aspects of language: *receptive language*, or understanding what others are communicating to you; *expressive language*, or conveying to others what you mean; and *pragmatics*, the practical and social aspects of language. Pragmatics include socially shared rules and expectations for how language is used, along with strategies for changing your use of language as the situation warrants. *Semantics*, which relates to the meanings and use of words, phrases, and sentences, may also be included.

Your SLP works on specific objectives in each session with your child and should be able to explain what the therapist and child have been working toward, along with what progress has been made. It's professional practice to set out written goals and objectives and to report in writing on progress. School districts require such documentation, but if you are paying out of pocket, you may have to ask your SLP for a plan and a report.

Getting something in writing is useful for your own knowledge, as a basis for talking with the SLP about progress and to share with the entire team.

Visually Based Communication Interventions

For children who find speech difficult, pictures, gestures, or sign language can aid the child's interaction in the moment while enabling further improvements in communication.

Because many people with autism are visual thinkers, Picture Exchange Communication System (PECS) and similar interventions can be effective. PECS was designed for children on the spectrum with delayed speech development. To learn its use, a child is given a set of pictures depicting favorite foods and toys. Every time the child seeks one of these items, he gives the corresponding picture to a parent, therapist, caregiver, or teacher who is serving as his communication partner. The partner hands the child the food or toy, and their exchange reinforces communication. PECS can also be used to communicate ideas and observations. For example, if a child sees a bird outside, he hands a picture of a bird to his communication partner. As the child increases his understanding of the value of communication, the thinking goes, he'll be enticed to do more and possibly begin to speak. PECS can increase the capacity for communication in children with ASDs (Flippin, Reszka, and Watson 2010).

Interventions That Target Social Interaction

People with autism can appear to live in another world. Drawing them into our world involves helping with language and communication, as we've just seen. Other interventions support social interaction in different ways. Perspective taking is one skill these aim to develop.

The Importance of Perspective Taking

How do you make sense of and account for other people's thoughts, feelings, and motivations? It turns out that understanding others' perspectives is a key to effective social interaction, because what you understand about other people shapes how you approach and interact with them.

Ingredients for Perspective Taking

Perspective taking is about ways of thinking, so the brain is involved. A part of the brain known as the *prefrontal cortex* is used in empathy and perspective taking. It's also involved in a cognitive capacity known as *theory of mind*, the ability to form mental models to account for other people's behavior (Baron-Cohen, Leslie, and Frith 1985). We don't yet know how brains differ and the implications for ASDs, but theory of mind research is promising.

Perspective taking also entails motivation. The interaction must be compelling enough to attract the required attention and effort. After all, we must expend effort to think about someone else and adapt what we say and do accordingly. For someone with language deficits, it's hard work. Motivation is therefore an important ingredient. It's also likely that knowledge of the world and personal experience come into play. Both can be difficult to come by for people with autism.

Skills are also involved, from making and maintaining appropriate eye contact to cultivating the ability to read facial expressions in order to determine whether the other person understands what you are communicating. And in settings from the dinner table to the playground to choir practice, an ability to read social cues in a group is also crucial. Because none of these skills comes naturally to them, people with autism may need to develop their own "social dictionary" of rules, cues, and expressions to use in social interactions.

Tools for Increasing Social Skills

If children with autism benefit from systematic and explicit language instruction, the same is true of social skills. So, social skills and social cognition are also crucial areas on which to focus your interventions. Unfortunately, there's no equivalent of a speech and language therapist for social interaction. On the other hand, the social sphere is the main focus of most SLP interventions, so your child's work with an SLP will already include much to support her social development. Integrated educational approaches include social components. In fact, social interaction is at the core of DIR Floortime, RDI, and SCERTS.

Some specific interventions are worth considering too.

Building Joint Attention

Joint attention is the ability to connect with someone else, including nonverbally, around a shared experience, object, or event. It is fundamental to communication and social interaction. Parents and therapists can build joint attention and enable reciprocal, or back-and-forth, social interaction by playing with children in ways that draw and sustain their interest. This form of play delivers large benefits for children's development. ABA programs often target joint attention, and DIR puts it at the heart of the intervention. Overall, there's evidence in favor of building joint attention; an excellent starting point for consulting the evidence for this and other interventions is the American Speech-Language-Hearing Association's National Center for Evidence-Based Practice in Communication Disorders web resources on autism treatment (ncepmaps.org/ASD-Treatment-Cognition-Language.php).

Learning with and from Peers

Social skills groups. Practicing social skills with matched peers, with appropriate support and coaching, can help people with autism learn basic rules and strategies for handling common social situations. At their most successful, social skills groups reduce anxiety, increase interaction, improve behaviors preferred by peers and teachers, build flexibility, support perspective taking, and increase conversational skills. But overall findings on social skills groups are mixed, with some studies showing weak or inconsistent results, poor maintenance, or little generalization (Williams White, Keonig, and Scahill 2007). In keeping with what parents tell us, their value is difficult to predict, not least of all because the group itself can vary and because generalization is not easily supported. Parents also note that for some children, rule-based teaching can reinforce rigidity.

Peer-based interventions. By modeling, prompting, and coaching your child, typically developing classmates may be able to help him develop social skills (Zhang and Wheeler 2011), but the opportunities need to be carefully orchestrated and supported by staff.

Social Stories

Social stories are short, direct narratives that convey socially useful information. Families and teachers use them to prepare a child with autism for new experiences, manage anxiety, and address behavioral challenges. Usually very simply written, each story focuses on only one situation or interaction and aims to teach rules, norms, and procedures explicitly. For example, your child could have separate stories for meeting a new person, going on a class outing to a museum, taking a train, and going bowling. This technique is being shown to work (Quirmbach et al. 2009). To learn more and get ideas for writing your own social stories, see *The New Social Story Book*, by Carol Gray (Future Horizons, 2010). Social video modeling is another option to consider.

Teaching Perspective Taking

Direct and video instruction. Can you teach someone perspective taking by breaking it down into its elements? Researchers are investigating step-by-step techniques—for instance, helping a child correctly identify what another person can see (see, for example, Gould et al. 2011). Another approach uses videos of situations where a model correctly performs perspective-taking tasks. The video is stopped for questions about perspectives. When rewarded for correct responses, children with autism improve (LeBlanc et al. 2003). Not enough evidence exists that children carry over what is learned to other situations.

Mind Reading. Building on theory-of-mind research, a software program called Mind Reading has been shown to teach children to recognize basic and complex emotions in faces and voices (Golan and Baron-Cohen 2006).

Social thinking. Promising new approaches support skills and capabilities for thinking about other people and social interactions in the moment. A practical and comprehensive body of work on social thinking aimed at parents, teachers, and people with autism, from children to working adults, provides useful tools for improving social interaction. You can find materials on social thinking, such as Michelle Garcia Winner's "Think with Your Eyes" curriculum, at socialthinking.com, which also offers a variety of her excellent books. Initial assessments are encouraging (Crooke, Hendrix, and Rachman 2008), and new materials and studies continue to appear.

Social Facilitation

It's one thing to learn specific social skills in a structured group or via a story, but even the best teacher cannot cover all situations. And we know that social skills generalization is particularly difficult for people with autism. So, why not have a coach on hand right then and there, during the situation? The playground is an obvious opportunity to help build social skills in real-world settings. This approach may be called *in situ* or *in vivo social facilitation*, or *naturalistic skills teaching*. It makes a lot of sense, but there are several challenges: there is no standard approach or method to follow, and the research evidence is mixed (perhaps as a result).

Arts-Based Interventions

There are many other interventions to consider. To round out this survey, we'll take a quick look at music, art, dance, and other expressive therapies.

Music Therapy

Although music therapy is usually considered to be separate from speech therapy, music can be used to reinforce communication in other interventions. As a therapeutic intervention to improve social skills and communication in children with autism, music therapy has shown positive effects on spoken and gestural communication (Gold, Wigram, and Elefant 2006). It could be a valuable adjunct to other therapies and teaching, but it should not be the only tool used to address communication deficits.

Art, Dance, and Other Expressive Therapies

Other expressive therapies may function similarly to music therapy, but we still lack research evidence of their value. Remember that a lack of scientific findings doesn't mean that a given therapy is a bad idea. If you're interested in drawing on expressive therapies, consider combining the artistic and expressive elements with a more structured component that draws on the approaches or content in your child's school or home programs, for instance, linked to a language, social, or behavioral program. And don't forget to gather your own data using some of the assessment ideas at the end of chapter 7.

Learning about and getting by in the real world is the final major area of concern we'll address.

CHAPTER 12

Real-Life Knowledge, Skills, and Families

What can you do today to help your child be able to someday strike up a conversation with strangers easily and appropriately? What will enable her to ride a bus, shop for groceries, or make her bed? In this chapter, we present some practical suggestions for helping your child learn about and get by in the world.

We start by looking at practical general knowledge, because although not often discussed by experts, it's crucial. Participating in the social world requires motivation, interaction skills, and language, as we've seen. It also requires a knowledge base including all sorts of information about how the world works, which your child may need to be taught explicitly. To take part in family, school, and community activities, it's also important that your child know the practical steps: what happens, in what sequence, and what she is supposed to do.

Then we look at effective methods of procedural instruction—how to teach your child with autism to do things like make a grilled cheese sandwich.

And at the end of it all, we'll share parent-tested, practical advice on handling challenges, focusing on the everyday stuff that can make a big difference for your child and your entire family.

Knowledge about the World

Educational programs for children with autism go beyond the purely academic in many ways. Thanks to behavioral therapists and other professionals, we know how to teach a child to get dressed. But educational programs fall short in other practical domains. It's much less clear how to teach about the world in general. Parents come up against this limitation when they realize that their child with an ASD is failing to pick up knowledge that others take for granted. This knowledge is difficult to impart with traditional methods.

People with autism who have gaps in their practical, general knowledge are at a disadvantage at school, in the community, and on the job. We're not talking about the stuff of TV quiz shows.

Think of all that *isn't* on any school syllabus but informs everything from small talk to enjoying movies to running errands to making sense of classroom discussions.

Practical Note:
What's Missing from Your Child's Knowledge of the World?

To give you a sense of what we mean, we asked parents of children on the autism spectrum what their children did *not* pick up. Here are some of their answers:

- What the tooth fairy is and why most kids care

- That the United States and Canada are both countries

- What a "bad guy" is

- That you first check your fridge and cupboard to make sure you have all the ingredients for dinner

- That Spanish is a language with a different word for pretty much everything

- That when you play a game, each team or player usually starts with a score of zero

- That at the dentist, you do not swallow the things they put in your mouth (unless you are told to)

- What war is and that both sides want to win

- That when you spill something messy, if you draw attention to it (for example, by exclaiming), someone will come and help

- That kids' pizza is usually plain cheese pizza

- That fries are made from potatoes and ketchup from tomatoes

- That if a scene in a movie or book focuses on an item or plot detail, it will matter later in the story

- That when you check your luggage on an airplane, you get it back at your destination

- What monsters are

- That in a kids' detective story, there will be a mystery and the protagonist will solve it

- That you have to pay for everything at the store

Other kids seem to absorb this stuff automatically. Parents of a child on the spectrum may not realize what their child doesn't know (as we learned from the family of a child who swallowed the dentist's cotton packing after an extraction). Of course, some things won't matter: your family may not care about the tooth fairy, and in any case she fades in importance for older children. Excellent teachers and therapists will always address gaps in knowledge they encounter. But many children need much more.

The Importance of Knowledge about the World

Practical knowledge about the world underpins much of what happens in school. Classroom teachers can't possibly teach every single aspect of a given topic to their students, so they rely on a level of general understanding in framing their instruction. Without this general knowledge, your child faces a disadvantage in the classroom.

Knowing some basic facts about the world is necessary for fun things too: getting the point of jokes, following stories, playing games. General knowledge enables everyday conversations and shared social experiences. If you think about it, every group of children has its own culture. Preschoolers' culture is linked to books, television shows, snack foods, characters that appear on their clothes and lunch bags, and, of course, the play experiences they enjoy. Typical kids learn all sorts of things from each other, as parents know, including rude words, what toy to ask for, and what television show to watch. In turn, they draw on this knowledge in social interactions. Knowing your own culture enables participation.

How Do Others Learn about the World?

Outside the classroom, most kids build knowledge of the world without anyone realizing it's happening: via errands, travel, outings; reading news stories; talking to friends and family; listening at the kitchen table. We even learn from commercials, because they are designed to telegraph key ideas. Our children with ASDs not only have less time for these things, but also may not enjoy them at all. Sensory, communication, and other challenges make it hard to take in and interpret new information in a busy store or at a crowded church function. Even if your child accompanies you on weekly errands, he may not pick up much from the experience. So, we're back to the question: how do we teach practical, general knowledge about the world?

Perhaps we can borrow from professional teachers who tackle the problem of uneven knowledge in regular-education classrooms. One approach is called *incidental teaching*: in covering a given topic, additional facts are taught as they come up. Another option is to use a simple structure for interactive learning: the teacher probes students to see what they already know, asking the class what they most want to learn. The teaching is then customized to build on what is already known, remedy gaps in knowledge, and connect to what motivates the children. Children on the autism spectrum benefit from more explicit, structured teaching, often at a slower pace (an unfortunate side effect is that less material fits into a given teaching session). Learners with autism may be less able to participate in typical classroom processes, such as discussing what they want to learn. Yet they may need to be taught more, so it's important to set learning goals appropriately, make the teaching as engaging as possible, and help children integrate and use what they are learning.

Develop Your Own Practical Learning Agenda

Customize a plan to fill in the gaps in your child's practical understanding of the world, selecting from these ideas.

Set the Learning Agenda

Start by looking at your child's current life to come up with ideas for what to probe and teach. If you think about it, your family's lived experience involves all sorts of opportunities to explore key facts about how the world works. Seasons and weather offer chances to teach vocabulary and discuss causality by asking such questions as, "Why do you wear rain boots?" and, "When and why do you prune in the garden?" They also let you talk about what's happening in the community or discuss holidays and all sorts of other events.

Probe for Initial Knowledge or Understanding

To customize your teaching, start by exploring your child's current knowledge. What does she already know? Depending on your child, this can be a bit like detective work. A nonverbal child can point to the right coat to wear or indicate a yes-or-no answer to a question. Your family likely has a good sense of what your child already knows, but it's wise to try to confirm it as you plan your "practical curriculum" for this sort of teaching. Getting confirmation needn't be too complex; depending on your child's communication skills, you may be able to use free-form conversations or a series of yes-or-no questions about the specifics you want to explore.

Now for some practical suggestions for creating your child's learning agenda from current experience.

Practical Note:
Four Ways to Build a Practical Knowledge Learning Agenda

Events are opportunities. Use community events, holidays, seasons, news, and other things happening in society, as well as school outings and family experiences, to generate ideas to explore. This is not as difficult as it seems: every week, select a theme from recent or upcoming events. In a few minutes you can list facts that you'd want your child to know. If your child is going to a bowling-alley birthday party, you could teach the steps in the game along with its goals. If there's an upcoming school outing to a museum for your middle schooler, the list might include what a museum looks like, knowing that there's a series of fantasy movies in which museum exhibits come alive for the night, developing a "Dos and Don'ts" list for how to behave, discussing what kinds of museums kids tend to like and what they might find boring, and maybe covering some basic facts about museums. And for Valentine's Day, you could discuss the date, what it means for children, and what people say and do on that day.

Find clues in daily experiences. Your child's daily life can provide ideas for what to teach. For a less verbal child, ask teachers, other family members, therapists, and others to look for any nuggets of needed knowledge that come up in the course of current experiences and schoolwork, including during school bus rides, TV watching, story reading, class projects, and so on. Have everyone who spends time or works with your child jot these items in a notebook that travels with him in his backpack. This incidentally generated list gives you ideas for what to explore with, and teach to, your child. The goal is to include nonacademic along with academic materials.

Use other kids for ideas. Tap into what other kids know, talk about, and do. Be a detective! An aide is a great source of information on this front.

Here, too, a notebook can come in handy. What do other kids your child's age or at his developmental level talk about, know, and take for granted? One family asked the paraprofessional working with their child to capture classmates' common expressions, topics of conversation, games, books, and TV shows of interest. They used the list to design their teaching, including some expressions and language that would help the child sound more like his peers.

Tap into your child's interests. Set aside time for your child to write or draw every day. These words or pictures provide a glimpse into what he makes of his own experiences, giving you an entry point for extending his practical knowledge. Choose an approach that will work: a daily afternoon assignment to generate three sentences, write five words, or draw a picture. One family convinced their child's teachers to photograph something unusual or highly motivating in their son's day and e-mail it to them by early afternoon every day. The family used the photos to spur interaction. They also provided clues for topics to explore with their child. Benefits of this strategy included building reporting skills and bolstering language use and interaction, while also helping you to customize an interest-based practical teaching plan.

Once you've come up with a great list of ideas and themes to explore with your child, the next step is teaching. You'll need to spark her interest, convey some specifics, and check retention and generalization.

Practical Teaching

We have suggestions for going from a list of potential ideas to specific teaching for your homegrown program. We've learned that your approach needs to be either extremely simple and predictable (do ten minutes of flash cards every day, for instance, and keep it simple) or else highly motivating and connected to an intense interest. This is "extra" work for both you and your child, so it needs to be feasible for the entire family. It may make sense to do something routine and simple for the school year, saving special projects for school vacations if you have more time then.

Practical Note:
Four Teaching Strategies

Make your own flash cards. Create flash cards with a question on one side and an answer on the other. You can use them to teach basic facts or define words. If you follow a consistent format, this is something you build on over time. Some children with autism love to interact with collections of materials, especially if it's personally meaningful. You could store all of your flash cards in a box or an album, giving your child material to browse through later. You could use the same information to create slide presentations, if you have access to computer software like PowerPoint and it's the sort of thing your child (and you!) enjoy. Here, too, it's useful to have a simple format. Once you have a setup that works, it's easy to create a weekly set of materials and then do a little work with your child every day. One family used a couple of hours every Sunday to create a new slide deck that included facts and pictures, and then reviewed the material over the week, adding to it or editing it as needed. By the end of the week, there was a simple slide show that the child had mastered and could review on screen or print out to share.

Engage in creative projects. For some children, more complex projects are motivating. Eight-year-old Anna loved dioramas, turning shoe boxes into detailed scenes created from materials around the house. Her family created an "art bin" for scrap materials: corks, packing material, samples of fabrics, straws, and catalogs with lots of pictures to cut out. With help from her parents, Anna used these materials to create dioramas. The family used the joint activity to target learning goals by incorporating informal, incidental instruction about common facts and general knowledge into their interactions as they collaborated on the projects. For instance, Anna wanted to build a model of a coffee shop. As her parents helped, they discussed beverages for children and adults, how the ordering process works, whether doughnuts are a healthy food, and the flow of money in a purchase transaction. Labels summarized key facts that her parents wanted Anna to retain. She would present the diorama to family visitors, a further chance for interaction.

Make your own books. Simple books can help children master basic information and may even work for toddlers. One mother bought small, inexpensive photo albums (sometimes called brag books) on clearance at her local store. Into each left-hand page, she slipped a picture: something she'd snapped with her mobile phone or printed from a web search, taken from a magazine or catalog, or culled from picture books picked up in a bookstore bargain bin. On the right-hand pages, she wrote key words, a phrase, or a sentence for her young child. Her child brought the books on outings and looked at them at home. Over the course of a year, the mother created books on pirates, fans, swimming, and breakfast. The books conveyed vocabulary while teaching general facts and serving as the basis for interaction with teachers and caregivers. Her preschooler loved looking at the special books again and again.

Storybooks created around a child's experiences can also prove to be motivating. An easy way to assemble a book is to insert page protectors into inexpensive binders. Stationery stores carry "presentation books," with covers you can customize and plastic sleeves for your pages of text. Relatives and babysitters of Chris, a young boy with autism, helped build a library of special narrative books for him. They wrote books about holidays and seasons, cats, and Africa. Each topic related to their interactions with the boy. His grandmother sent a simple storybook she'd written about Christmas. The book was based on catalog images. To make it fun, Grandma glued a cutout picture of the boy onto each page. Chris got the book in the mail before his family made the trip to visit his grandmother. Bringing it along helped him prepare for the visit and learn some basic facts about Christmas that he had not yet picked up. For his grandmother, who sometimes struggled to interact with Chris, the book helped spark conversation. Important for her, the experience enabled the two to share the holiday experience, something she liked to do with all of her grandchildren.

Customize a game. Another strategy is to take a game your child has mastered and change it to incorporate basic facts and information you want him to learn. Some games don't even need to be changed—think of such guessing games as Twenty Questions. In other cases, you can modify board games. Why not create a version of a trivia game to teach facts? One family took the game Guess Who? and pasted photos of the child's classmates into each square, adding details about each child that would both teach some information and help set the stage for social interaction.

Checking for Learning

We mentioned checking for existing knowledge and interest at the outset of your teaching effort. Once you've spent a week or two teaching your child about, say, a religious holiday, the World Series in baseball, or all the terms we use for various denominations of money, you'll want to test what he has learned and uses. The most natural way to do this is incidentally, when the right moment comes up in your lives. Some parents ask others to bring up a given topic (for example, suggest that Uncle Bill talk to the child about the World Series).

The same general approaches your child's teaching team uses to generalize and retain learning can also apply to informal and practical teaching, but despite the value of gathering data to test learning, it may not be feasible to formally assess this aspect of your child's education. Nevertheless, look for any evidence that your child has *not* retained what you were trying to teach. A simple tactic is to ask your child's school team whether he's using the vocabulary, ideas, or other material you've worked on at home.

If the teaching doesn't seem to sink in, it might mean that you're going too fast, setting the level too high, making your sessions too long, or failing to mesh with your child's interests. It may simply take longer than you expect for your child to integrate new material into his daily life and draw on it in interactions. Pare it back to something you can easily do every day. If you can work with only one hand-drawn flash card a day, so be it. Over the course of a year, you'll have exposed your child to hundreds of facts; that's a significant amount of information!

Simple tools like flash cards used daily allow you to check whether your child is retaining the instruction; every month or so, pull out some previously used cards to review with your child. You could quiz him, invent a game, or even find a way to connect the two activities with each other. The third of these suggestions relates to our last point about teaching practical, general knowledge about how the world works.

Connecting the Learning to Make It Meaningful

Memorizing individual facts is not enough. How do they all fit together, and how does it all relate to life? People with autism may arrange information in their minds differently from the way others do. This may bring benefits; we've yet to understand how talents and genius may flow from the different ways that people with autism think. But to get by in the world, it's important to connect and draw on ideas and information to solve both academic and practical problems as they arise. If your teenager teaches herself about color theory, maybe she'll eventually tap into this knowledge for further study, a hobby, or even professionally; that's great. But she also needs to learn what colors are considered okay for her to wear to school and then choose appropriate clothing, or how to eat healthfully by including foods of different colors.

To carry over and use what she is learning, your child can share with others topical materials that she has created. She could bring her own books, pictures, or art projects to a social interaction. The tangible object (or media, if the project is on a computer, phone, or other device) provides something specific that everyone can refer to. This technique can work even when spoken communication is difficult, because partners in the interaction can make comments that create opportunities for your child to respond nonverbally.

Practical Note:
Three Ways to Embed the Learning

Injecting the practical learning agenda into the entire family's frame of reference enables incidental teaching; develops, extends, and connects ideas; and builds social interaction. Our final set of practical suggestions builds on this idea.

Create a family bulletin. One family's weekly e-mail to their son's team flagged ideas, vocabulary, and knowledge that they asked others to draw on. Another family installed a blackboard next to the kitchen table. Key ideas went on the board, and everyone who came to the house would work references to the ideas into their interactions—not only with the child who had autism, but also in their conversations with each other. This gave the children multiple exposures to key material, generated natural variation in language and terminology, and showed how the ideas were related to many different things, all of which deepened the learning.

Link home and school. Find ways to tap into opportunities at school, if it's feasible. We suggested sending materials to school for sharing with your child's peers or the entire class. You can define special projects. A therapist working with Yasmeen, a second grader who found it difficult to talk to her typical peers during recess and lunch, created a simple interview guide to structure conversations with classmates. Her interviews had a goal: she asked each person about pets. At home, they created a chart depicting pets belonging to children in that class. In this case, the project tapped into special interests (she loved cats), taught her some general knowledge (she learned about dogs and pets in general), reinforced her math curriculum (she was learning to display numerical data), and built her language and social interaction skills while shoring up peer relationships.

Talk it out. Encourage everyone around your child to narrate their everyday thoughts and actions. This connects the topical facts you have been teaching your child to his experiences with you. If you've been teaching about Halloween and are now taking the kids to buy a pumpkin, narrate your thought process during the entire outing. Start by talking about where you're going and why. Aim not so much to tell as to narrate your internal thought process, as a model of sorts that explains how you make decisions, adapt plans, and solve problems. In the Halloween example, this might mean that when you arrive at the pumpkin display, you talk through your decision process. "This one has great color, but it's too small," you might say. "Oh, there's no stem on this one. I think that would make it hard to take the top off." Even if your child does not join the conversation in the moment, this can help him learn. A useful strategy for eliciting your child's input is to combine narration with comments that elicit a response. For example, you might say, "This pumpkin is so bumpy...," and then wait, in case he says something in response, as you examine a bumpy gourd next to a smooth one. Placing the facts, vocabulary, and cultural knowledge that you have been teaching in context by drawing on them in the course of your daily lives is a great way to make the learning agenda meaningful.

These ideas are just a starting point. Doubtless, you and your family will come up with your own useful strategies for all three aspects of teaching practical, general knowledge about the world. If one method doesn't work, try something else. Tap into your team and family for ideas.

Daily Living Skills

In many ways, the real stuff of every family's life is the tasks, chores, and everyday activities that get you out the door in the morning, put a meal on the table (and into stomachs), or get the children into bed. We'll share some ideas for how to help your child build appropriate skills for daily living.

First of all, let's acknowledge that with a developmentally delayed child, there's no checklist to tell you what she should be able to do by a given age. Your child may have great abilities in some domains and struggle to master others. It took one family many difficult months to teach their preschooler to wash his hands, even though he had already, completely on his own, built a habit of putting every book away in the right place as soon as he'd finished with it.

With a child on the autism spectrum, we've seen some families settle into habits that turn into ruts. Unlike her typical peers, your child may not wake up one day asking to make her own breakfast or insisting on choosing her clothes. You may have fewer possibilities for negotiating with your child about responsibilities and chores. When typical children ask for a new privilege, parents use the opportunity to set new goals: yes, they may tell a ten-year-old, "We can talk about getting a pet once you show us that you can be responsible by taking out the trash without our having to ask you every day."

What if your child never asks for new privileges? Goals for increased independence may come from your family's (and educational team's) aspirations for your child's participation in school, family, and community life. If your elementary-school kid can use the bathroom on her own, more options for school and social life open up to her. A twelve-year-old who cannot blow her nose encounters more difficulty in an inclusion setting, and when she has allergies, her parents may be more likely to keep her at home.

At the same time, there's no question that trying to get a child to master skills beyond her abilities not only is a waste of time, but also can disappoint the team and frustrate the child. Use your team to set appropriate goals and make sure they are aligned with what's important for your family.

Practical Note:
Daily Living Skills

The practical skills for getting by in the world are often called ADLs (activities of daily living) or DLS (daily living skills). The following list gives some examples:

- Shampooing

- Tying shoelaces

- Taking a bus ride

- Choosing an appropriate coat, putting it on, and buttoning or zipping it

- Clearing the table

- Taking daily medications

- Folding laundry

- Checking the expiration date on food in the supermarket

- Downloading music or finding a movie online

Strategies for teaching specific skills and activities depend on your child's profile and needs, as well as the tasks themselves. To convey some of the options, let's look at one practical example.

Practical Note:
A Sample Program for Teaching a Child to Make the Bed

First, define the goal very specifically; for example, "We want Jamal to make his bed every morning before he leaves his room, without having to be asked." Decide what you mean by "making the bed": how neat does it need to be? A fun approach is to take photographs of the bed in various states of disarray (perhaps using a mobile phone). Working with the child, categorize the bed in each picture as "good enough" or "not good enough."

Next, map the steps in the process. Start by specifying the time and place: "After you get dressed in the morning, before you leave your room." List each step in the process of making the bed. Write down every detail. It helps to actually carry out the process with a collaborator. Include instructions for what to do if things go wrong; for example, "If you pull back the covers and notice that the bottom sheet is untucked, tuck it in," or "If you can't find the pillow, check under the bed." Your child may be a partner in this step.

Now that you have documented each step in excruciating detail, simplify your list. Can you combine steps? Leave some out? Set aside others for later? The goal is to construct the simplest possible set of instructions that is both complete and tailored to your child's capabilities. It's a good idea to write them out, even if your child will be using drawings or images. Test your instructions by getting someone else to follow them literally. End your sequence with the step that you want your child to take next; for example, "Turn off the light and come to breakfast." If it makes sense to do so, include a step to have your child check his result against the goal (in our example, Jamal could compare his bed with the "good enough" images, repeating the sequence if his bed resembles a "not good enough" image).

Translate your instructions into language or images that work for your child. Your child may initially need someone next to him to convey the steps, using your notes as a script, and possibly to guide the physical action. Another child may be able to use materials independently. Regardless, instructions need to be calibrated to what works for your child. For Jamal's bed-making program, the family knew that multistep instructions beginning with "if" would be too complex. Instead, they created simple directives: "Pull back the covers. Is the bottom sheet tucked in? Yes → next step. No → tuck in the sheet at the bottom, sides, and top of the bed."

Design materials that your child will use to learn the full sequence of steps. Options include:

- Clearly numbered index cards with a phrase on each.

- Laminated cards on a ring or lanyard, with an image and a few words on each.

- A poster on the wall, with step-by-step photos.

- A spiral-bound book with stiff pages that can stand on a counter (reuse an old book; simply paste sheets describing steps onto existing pages).

- A single sheet of written instructions, placed in a page protector.

- A laminated checklist and a dry-erase marker for checking off steps.

- A simple verbal reminder that summarizes the steps. For example, you could create a memorable acronym (for the bed-making sequence, the phrase "putt putts" could remind Jamal to *pu*ll back the covers, *t*uck in the sheets, *pu*ll up the covers, *t*op off with his pillow, and *s*mooth the bed).

- A social story depicting the steps in the process that features your child or a favorite character. You may also need to refer to explicit, step-by-step instruction, but the story can help address anxiety, present the reasons why it is good to work on this skill, and place it in a social context.

- A video of the entire process, perhaps starring a cousin or friend that your child is drawn to. This can teach the physical steps and the sequence and even show how to use a written guide.

Now that you have a plan, the real work starts. You'll likely start with some direct teaching (during which you may realize that you need to refine the materials; it's all part of the process). For children with fewer abstract thinking skills or who feel anxious, make the run-through as fun as possible. It may help to introduce the goals and rationale *after* you've gone through the program, once the child has a sense of the task at hand. Depending on your child's developmental level, negotiate the criteria: does he need to make his bed on his own every single day? Are Sundays "free days"? Does he get one "pass" a week? Is there a reward at the end? Your child may find a tangible reward motivating; for others, a social reward works, such as calling a relative to report performance. Depending on your child, there may be interim rewards, or you may set a longer-term goal, such as a full week of independent bed-making.

The final part of the process is increasing independence and checking that performance is maintained. His parents wanted ten-year-old Ben to dress himself. They began by helping with each step of the process during the first week, pointing to items and using verbal instructions that reinforced the information on a poster they had made for his bedroom wall. In the second week, they pointed to the items. In the third week, they simply gestured to the instructions, and in the fourth week they only checked his performance at the end of the sequence. Every day, using a chart on his bedroom wall, Ben indicated that he had completed all steps in the process, and it was gratifying for the entire family to see the line of check marks growing every day. At the end of the month, Ben had mastered the goal, and he continued to dress himself. His family left step-by-step instructions on the wall in his bedroom for a few months and then took the poster down.

Not all attempts to teach activities for daily living skills will work as smoothly for every family, and in Ben's case, they had struggled with hand-washing when he was four. Perhaps this was why the family waited so long to work on his skill in getting dressed. Ben's family felt that his getting dressed on his own was less critical to his participation in school and the community than hand-washing had been. It was a choice that worked for that family. In the next section, we turn to some common everyday challenges in living with a child who has autism.

Everyday Challenges

Parents of children with autism deal with the usual parenting responsibilities: toilet training, diet, sleep, personal hygiene, chores, and homework, to name a few. It may take your child longer than usual to achieve milestones, and you may need to try different routes to get there. You may redefine goals, setting your own special milestones for your child.

Along the way, you may encounter things that typical families rarely have to deal with: severe behavioral challenges or self-injury, for instance. Parents tell us that everything can seem calm for a while, but then there's a phase when multiple things go badly. Sometimes you know what's to blame: developmental shifts, or a change in medication or at school. Other times it may just be a mystery. Either way, you can't ignore the challenges. You have to address each head on, in some way or another.

To offer some help, we'll take a quick look at toilet training, diet, and sleep, listing some factors that may affect these areas for your child and outlining a few suggestions. We conclude the chapter with some advice for handling behavioral and other challenges, linking our discussion to ideas we've been developing throughout the book. But first we have a question for you.

Practical Note:
Is It Really a Problem?

If you're wrestling with a potential problem with your child's behavior, remember that ultimately, what matters most is your child and your family. Consider these questions with an open mind: *Why is this issue important? Is it dangerous? Is our family life made difficult and unpleasant? Does it prevent my child from learning? Is it socially unacceptable? Inconvenient?* After all, some behaviors that seem problematic in one setting would not be seen as problems in other settings or if the child were younger. The burly teenager who gives everyone hugs is an example. Of course, he should learn that it is socially unacceptable to hug strangers. Some families may have a more lax approach to his hugging acquaintances, whereas to other families, this behavior would be seen as a real problem. Tackle what matters most to your family and your child, taking into account the advice of your medical and educational teams.

Toilet Training, Eating, and Sleeping

We'll consider three areas parents often ask about.

Toilet Training

Your child with autism may take longer than most kids do to learn to use the toilet. Not all children with ASDs make the transition to independent toilet use. Do not assume that a lack of understanding or motivation is the barrier. Toilet training requires motor coordination along with body awareness, known as *proprioception*. Sensory underreactivity could mean that your child does not feel the sensation of needing to go to the toilet. Or the sensations, sights, sounds, smells, or textures associated with going to the toilet could be unbearable. Constipation or diarrhea pose extra challenges.

What works with toilet training? Above all, patience. Try a basic behavioral strategy: Keep careful notes on when, where, and how your child goes to the toilet. Use them to develop a plan of action based on your observations. Be reassuring and never punish for mistakes. Consult a book on the subject or a therapist for more ideas.

Diet

People on the spectrum may limit the range of foods they eat. Some can eat apparently unlimited quantities of a given food, such as tomatoes, necessitating that the food be kept under lock and key! Sensory responses can lead to extreme reactions to certain tastes, food smells, and textures; temperature may play a role too. For children who do not eat enough, hunger awareness may be an issue. Communication problems make it difficult to express the need for food or to discuss what aspects are unpalatable. Food allergies could cause discomfort.

Forget the outdated strategy of withholding a child's next meal until the present one is eaten. And mealtime fights and drama are likely to worsen problems. In general, it's wise to let your child control what she eats, once you've offered her a selection of healthy foods.

But if there's a medical reason or another reason to shape food consumption, the first step is to document what, when, where, and how your child eats. Be the observer! Note sensory issues such as textures, temperature, smell, and taste. A child who won't tolerate a food one way may eat it in another form. Served raw, a carrot may be too crunchy and noisy to bite into, but puréed, it's okay. Some parents use social stories featuring a child's favorite character trying new food. Be open to the possibility that the child's tastes will change or that they don't fit normal expectations. Who would have guessed that a kid who would not eat hamburgers would love fried clams?

Sleep

Sleep problems can affect children with autism, and it's easy to think of the negative effects this could have on your child. But if he isn't sleeping, you likely aren't either. Try some specific changes. Double-check evening medications, foods, and drinks for stimulants that could keep him awake. Establish a calming bedtime routine, and set an early cutoff for video games, computers, TV, and even cell phones, because their light is known to interrupt sleep. Ask your doctor about the advisability of melatonin, a supplement that helps adjust sleep and waking cycles and is frequently used with good effect with ASD kids who have difficulty falling asleep, staying asleep, or waking too early. It is usually well tolerated with minimal side effects.

Behavioral Difficulties

Imagine a world that bombards you with sensory input and external demands beyond your abilities to manage. It sounds like torture. Living with autism can feel like that, particularly when illness, medication, puberty, or changes at school or at home add extra challenges. The result can be extremes of behavior that leave a family feeling powerless and frustrated. There may be no simple answers, but there are strategies to try in such situations.

Practical Note:
Fifteen Strategies for Addressing Behavioral Difficulties

Use reinforcements. A basic behavioral approach to reduce interfering or undesirable behaviors is to withhold desired reinforcement every time problematic behaviors occur. This is tricky to do, because it must happen immediately and involves not doing something. If you withhold reinforcement for poor behavior, make sure to reward appropriate behavior.

Investigate. Use your observational skills to track what you see and hear along with the details: where, when, duration, conditions, anything that might be a factor. Have your team examine the data to come up with ideas for what to try next. To analyze behaviors more systematically, use the A-B-C approach.

Use A-B-C charting. A technique borrowed from behavior analysis equips you to assess what might be giving rise to, or even reinforcing, problematic behavior. There are three things to capture:

Antecedent: What came first? Note the time and situation, along with events that have just taken place.

Behavior: Describe what your child actually did (be careful to focus on the behavior itself, not your interpretation of it). Include duration (for example, "She screamed for forty-five seconds").

Consequence: What happened next, as a result? This can include natural consequences (her playdate partner ran out of the room) or what you as parents did next.

Record your observations in an A-B-C chart to pinpoint possible causes of interfering or undesirable behavior. Graphing numerical data can help you see patterns. Your team can help you make sense of the data and suggest appropriate strategies to try.

Find motivators. Social motivators, such as others' approval, are tools you can use to shape behavior in typically developing children, but these don't necessarily work for children with autism. Borrow techniques that work for your child in other areas, such as the classroom, to motivate performance and self-management. Consider developing social stories that feature motivating characters. Rewards that tap into your child's special interests may work.

Provide behavioral support. Positive behavioral support can reduce problem behavior and improve quality of life. It starts with a functional assessment (mentioned in chapter 10); think of a stepped-up A-B-C. The resulting plan aims to identify and remove triggers of poor behavior, support anything that enables desirable behavior, teach the child better alternatives to problem behavior, and reward improvements.

Build skills for daily living. Teaching daily life skills may prevent or reduce everyday challenges. A child who can do more for herself needs less help. Mornings and bedtime may be easier for your family once your child brushes her own teeth. It can be a long process; know that sometimes, when your child is under stress, recently acquired skills disappear. Don't panic; when stress lifts, skills often reappear.

Design the layout. Physical supports can enable independence. Take a lesson from specialized classrooms: design and lay out what's needed to carry out a given task in a way that supports your child's completion of the required steps. Homework, the bathroom, and the kitchen offer potential opportunities.

Shore up functional communication. Another prevention strategy is to tackle key developmental needs with teaching and appropriate supports. Language is the obvious domain: children who can communicate better have fewer challenging behaviors. Frustration with sensory and communication difficulties may underlie some of the most vexing problems, including self-injurious behavior.

Using pictorial or written supports may guide and help manage anxiety for children with ASDs. Parents report that communication and planning supports (such as schedules) can be phased out as children internalize them and come to understand the general scheme of things.

Encourage self-management. To improve social behavior, your team can devise a system for rewarding your child based on an ongoing tally of her desired behaviors. She may learn to assess herself at moments that could otherwise become problematic. Self-assessment techniques may help children regulate themselves.

Build executive function capabilities. Children use planning and management skills to organize and manage their belongings and tasks. These skills, which relate to a capacity known as executive function, can be taught using a customized approach; consult an expert or a book.

Prepare. Changes in routines can be difficult. For some, knowing what to expect makes it tolerable, and schedules can help. A child who can't read may be able to interpret photographs or pictures arrayed in a grid or pasted onto a calendar. Some families draw up schedules on the fly, using paper or a portable whiteboard. If your child is starting a new school or visiting a new doctor, it might help to drive by the building and walk around it beforehand. Social stories can also help manage change.

Plan for travel. When it comes to travel, disruption in sleep and diet, along with new sensory environments, adds to the challenges. If you do not know how your child will react to a shift in routine, start small. Try a night in a local hotel or a sleepover at a friend's house to see what happens.

Prepare your child for a trip by showing pictures of the relative's house you plan to visit or photos of the hotel (websites where travelers post their own pictures offer better previews than hotel materials). Find a children's book about the destination and read it with your child ahead of time. Another idea is to ask other families or search online forums to learn about ASD-friendly locations. Some parks and attractions make special provisions to cater to children with alternative needs. If you have concerns, check with an airline, airport, or destination site ahead of time.

Check for safety and security. When you travel or take outings, ensure that your child has identification that includes a way to reach you (for a fee, a bracelet or card associated with a toll-free service can connect you with anyone calling on your child's behalf). This can give you some peace of mind as you head into the crowds at an airport or a theme park. At home, it's wise to call your local emergency services now, before anything ever happens, to let them know that a child with autism lives in your house. Training of first responders in the basics of interacting with people who have autism is on the increase.

Manage challenges as they arise. It's not always possible to plan to avoid problems when you have a child who cannot handle something like standing in lines. You may need to spring into action when you encounter a challenging situation. Don't be afraid to advocate for your family in the moment, by going to an agent or official and letting him know about your child's needs and verbal abilities. Be ready to do this by preparing a quick verbal explanation. Consider carrying a note (possibly from your child's doctor) that you have prepared ahead of time.

Reframe your own thinking. Every parent can use our last piece of advice. When the going gets tough, remember that your child does the best she can, given her particular circumstances. After all, nobody can do more than is possible for them at that moment. Rarely does anyone make failure a goal. If we understand that most people are trying to succeed, we tend to be more forgiving. Your child does her best—amid challenges that the rest of the world doesn't even understand.

Afterword

The pages you've been reading are loaded with many ideas. We hope they come in handy, both now and in the years to come. As we finished putting it all together for you, we reflected on our own experience to identify four things we learned along the way. Because we try to incorporate them into our own lives every day, we thought we'd share them with you.

Cultivate a habit of mindfulness. One of the most powerful practices you can build into your daily life is to be mindful. Mindfulness is the capacity to be present, paying attention to everything that's happening in a nonjudgmental way. Imagine what might happen in the following situation. Your child is trying to interact with you, but you are distracted with your own thoughts about a frustrating disagreement you had with your boss at work. You'd be squandering what might be a rare opportunity to engage your child in conversation, learn about what's on his mind, and build a more meaningful relationship with him. Developing the capacity to focus attention on what's going on here and now is a gift to yourself and others.

Speaking personally, we've learned that all too often we can be distracted from being present in the moment by thinking of other things. And life throws distractions at each of us on a regular basis! We've come to realize that there's no substitute for incorporating into our daily lives the practice of being present, doing one thing at a time, while trying to shake off our tendency to reach conclusions on the fly. Mindfulness helps us manage through our sometimes-chaotic lives and makes our relationships with others more meaningful and effective.

A mindful perspective can help you put into practice the aphorism we've all heard but often forget, that you can never really know what another's experience is. We can all be kinder and more generous in our thoughts about others.

One of the key differences of autism lies in how people think and process information. Understanding this has changed the way we see the world. Every day, when mindfulness fails us, we base dozens of off-the-cuff judgments on our instantaneous observations of others' behaviors and appearance. And, often without our knowing it, assessments that we form of others affect how we explain things to ourselves, including the motivations, intelligence, and like-mindedness we ascribe to other people. Our evaluations of others shape how we treat them.

It's easy to assume that someone who is slow to answer a question has nothing worthwhile to say. It's easy to assume that someone who looks different or speaks differently from us, hops and flaps a bit, or talks about train schedules in unusual detail has little in common with us, and maybe even that we should therefore have little to do with that person. Our assumptions exert a potent but invisible influence.

Snap judgments can be invaluable: they enable action in emergencies, for instance, and they are thought to be connected with instinct. But such judgments, we suspect, also lie behind prejudice, and they hamper our ability to make the most of our society's wonderful diversity of culture, experience, background, abilities, and skills, not to mention neurodiversity, or variation in ways of perceiving and thinking about the world. For us, the antidote is the practice of mindfulness and to remind ourselves how much we value acting respectfully.

We also think it's important to seize opportunities for open conversations with family, friends, or colleagues that help others loosen their snap judgments a bit and avoid reinforcing prejudice. Every day we try to remind ourselves to be present and slow the rush to judgment. Let's take our time and pay attention to what's actually happening, just like some of the people we know with autism.

Define, gather, and pay attention to the data. Mindfulness may appear to have little to do with the scientific method, but hear us out on this. Evidence-based approaches involve paying attention to the data. We think it's important to do this in many ways, by focusing on what's happening in the moment—that's the mindfulness—and by noticing our own reactions, thoughts, and judgments. Paying attention also includes carefully observing and listening to your child. Remember our advice to separate observations from attributions? The idea comes into play here and can be incredibly valuable when you are trying to sort out a problem in your child's life and make sense of what others are reporting to you about your child's behavior and performance.

And, of course, data includes the published scientific evidence you'd turn to, in order to choose a therapeutic or educational approach that's known to work widely. Paying attention to data also includes measuring and tracking behaviors and other things in your child's life; this process is invaluable for assessing whether or not a new treatment you're trying is working. Your own data is also essential for untangling behavioral puzzles. An A-B-C chart provides an approach you can implement at home.

Paying attention to the data can help you to be more accepting of what you learn from your child and the world. It can enable you to identify what doesn't work more quickly than you would otherwise, so it's more efficient than the alternative. And gathering data and really paying attention to what it says may also make it easier to accept the times when what you thought or expected turns out to be wrong.

Accept and appreciate your child while taking action and advocating. As parents, we accept and appreciate each child while also pushing for change, development, and progress. It's a testament to our ability to hold on to somewhat contradictory ideas at the same time. "I love you unconditionally," we say, "but you must (clean your room, go to sleep, finish your homework assignment), or else..."

Parents of children with autism are likely familiar with this contradiction. We want our children to feel surrounded with our love, and we want the world to accept each child for who she is. At the same time, we push our children to change in many ways: there are preschoolers who work over fifty hours a week in educational and therapeutic programming, and middle schoolers who spend three times as long as their classmates on homework every day. We coach our kids on the spectrum in the countless ways they need to change in order to fit in and get by in the world.

Where do we draw the line? Should the world change to accommodate people with autism, or should we continue to push for the treatments that enable them to change so that they can fit in with the world? Voices from within the autism community are reminding us of how important it is to accept and accommodate and to appreciate different ways of thinking. We also know how important it is to deliver treatments and therapies that reduce suffering and help people connect with the world in meaningful ways.

When it comes to advocating, we see several roles for parents. Learn about your child's specific needs and advocate on her behalf with the schools, other institutions, and your community. Advocate for the needs of everyone in the family, including yourself. And in society as a whole, advocate for needed research and resources, and for a reduction in the stigma and prejudice that make it difficult for someone with autism to participate fully in opportunities outside the home.

Tap into your own resilience and build solidarity in the world for all of us. You are resilient, maybe more than you realize. Throughout history, people have faced challenges that they would have predicted to be unbearable yet managed to survive. Some even emerge stronger. While we strive to reduce needless suffering, it's heartening to know that people are resilient and adaptable.

Many families of children with autism draw on this resilience to build a new family life with unconventional and unique aspects to it. And while "quirky" may sound good, let's not pretend that this new life is without its losses, in terms of diminished hopes and dreams for your child, along with the financial, emotional, and other costs that a diagnosis of autism entails.

But we're often amazed at how families of children with autism remake themselves, with new roles, new arrangements, and new trade-offs. Parents may discover new callings (one of your authors did!). Siblings, even as they are deprived of some aspects of a typical childhood, develop perspectives and capabilities that can serve them well. We'd like to celebrate the uniqueness of families like yours. We appreciate the inventiveness, courage, and persistence it takes to come up with the arrangements that make sense for your family. We want to help support your efforts to learn as much as you can and make the best decisions for your child and your family.

And we'd like to build some solidarity with you fellow parents as you find your family's new way forward. We'll know each other when we see you in the world. You may be taking your tall teenager onto the plane during preboarding "for families traveling with small children." Maybe that's you bringing your son into the women's room at the mall, pacing in the theater lobby with your child while everyone else is enjoying the show, or asking for two sets of crayons at the family restaurant because the first set will, inevitably, be broken into many tiny pieces instantly. Your child may be the one who always bolts straight into every bedroom and gets into every bed whenever you visit a new house, regardless of how inappropriate that is. Or yours could be the kid who drinks from strangers' water glasses at restaurants. Let's say hello and let's make sure to help each other out as we can, even if it's just by sticking up for each other or pretending that some of these things are really not so weird. And even these small acts can make the world a better place for our children.

Recommended Reading

Anderson, K., and V. Forman, eds. 2010. *Gravity Pulls You In: Perspectives on Parenting Children on the Autism Spectrum.* Bethesda, MD: Woodbine House.

Ariel, C. N., and R. A. Naseef, eds. 2006. *Voices from the Spectrum: Parents, Grandparents, Siblings, People with Autism, and Professionals Share Their Wisdom.* London: Jessica Kingsley Publishers.

Grandin, T. 2011. *The Way I See It: A Personal Look at Autism and Asperger's* Second Edition, Expanded edition. Arlington, TX: Future Horizon.

Gray, C. 2010. *The New Social Story Book: Over 150 Social Stories that Teach Everyday Social Skills to Children with Autism or Asperger's Syndrome, and Their Peers.* Rev. and expanded ed. Arlington, TX: Future Horizons.

National Autistic Society. 2010. "Real-Life Stories." London: The National Autistic Society. www.autism.org.uk/living-with-autism/real-life-stories .aspx.

Senator, S. 2010. *The Autism Mom's Survival Guide (for Dads, Too!): Creating a Balanced and Happy Life While Raising a Child with Autism.* Boston: Trumpeter.

Shore, S. M. 2003. *Beyond the Wall: Personal Experiences with Autism and Asperger Syndrome,* Second Edition. Shawnee Mission, KS: Autism Asperger Publishing Company.

Siegel, L. 2011. *The Complete IEP Guide: How to Advocate for Your Special Ed Child* Seventh Edition. Berkeley, CA: NOLO.

References

Abbeduto, L., M. M. Seltzer, P. Shattuck, M. Wyngaarden Krauss, G. Orsmond, and M. M. Murphy. 2004. "Psychological Well-Being and Coping in Mothers of Youths with Autism, Down Syndrome, or Fragile X Syndrome." *American Journal of Mental Retardation* 109 (3):237–54.

Allen, J. G., P. Fonagy, and A. W. Bateman. 2008. *Mentalizing in Clinical Practice*. Arlington, VA: American Psychiatric Publishing.

Allik, H., J. O. Larsson, and H. Smedje. 2006. "Health-Related Quality of Life in Parents of School-Age Children with Asperger Syndrome or High-Functioning Autism." *Health and Quality of Life Outcomes* 4:1.

American Psychiatric Association (APA). 2000. *Diagnostic and Statistical Manual of Mental Disorders: DSM-IV-TR*. 4th ed., text rev. Arlington, VA: American Psychiatric Publishing.

American Speech-Language-Hearing Association (ASHA). 2006. "Autism: Benefits of Speech-Language Pathology Services: What Do SLPs Do When Working with Individuals with Autism?" Accessed August 30, 2011. http://asha.org/public/speech/disorders/autismSLPbenefits.htm.

Anderson, L. T., M. Campbell, P. Adams, A. M. Small, R. Perry, and J. Shell. 1989. "The Effects of Haloperidol on Discrimination Learning and Behavioral Symptoms in Autistic Children." *Journal of Autism and Developmental Disorders* 19 (2):227–39.

Arking, D. E., D. J. Cutler, C. W. Brune, T. M. Teslovich, K. West, M. Ikeda, A. Rea, and A. Chakravarti. 2008. "A Common Genetic Variant in the Neurexin Superfamily Member CNTNAP2 Increases Familial Risk of Autism." *American Journal of Human Genetics* 82 (1):160–64.

Arnold, L. E., M. G. Aman, A. M. Cook, A. N. Witwer, K. L. Hall, S. Thompson, and Y. Ramadan. 2006. "Atomoxetine for Hyperactivity in Autism Spectrum Disorders: Placebo-Controlled Crossover Pilot Trial." *Journal of the American Academy of Child and Adolescent Psychiatry* 45 (10):1196–1205.

Ashwood, P., S. Wills, and J. van de Water. 2006. "The Immune Response in Autism: A New Frontier for Autism Research." *Journal of Leukocyte Biology* 80 (1):1–15.

Asperger, H. (1944) 1991. "Die 'Autistischen Psychopathen' im Kindesalter." ["Autistic Psychopathy in Childhood."] In German. In *Archiv fur Psychiatrie und Nervenkrankheiten* 177:76–137. Reprint in *Autism and Asperger Syndrome*, edited, translated, and annotated by U. Frith, 37–92, Cambridge, UK: Cambridge University Press. Citations refer to the Cambridge University Press edition.

Baron-Cohen, S. 2006. "The Hyper-Systemizing, Assortative Mating Theory of Autism." *Progress in Neuro-Psychopharmacology and Biological Psychiatry* 30 (5):865–72.

Baron-Cohen, S., E. Ashwin, C. Ashwin, T. Tavassoli, and B. Chakrabarti. 2009. "Talent in Autism: Hyper-Systemizing, Hyper-Attention to Detail and Sensory Hypersensitivity." *Philosophical Transactions of the Royal Society B* 364:1277–1383.

Baron-Cohen, S., A. M. Leslie, and U. Frith. 1985. "Does the Autistic Child Have a 'Theory of Mind'?" *Cognition* 21 (1):37–46.

Bayat, M. 2007. "Evidence of Resilience in Families of Children with Autism." *Journal of Intellectual Disability Research* 51 (9):702–14.

Bebko, J. M., M. M. Konstantareas, and J. Springer. 1987. "Parent and Professional Evaluations of Family Stress Associated with Characteristics of Autism." *Journal of Autism and Developmental Disorders* 17 (4):565–76.

Bertoglio, K., and R. L. Hendren. 2009. "New Developments in Autism." *Psychiatric Clinics of North America* 32 (1):1–14.

Buchsbaum, M. S., E. Hollander, M. M. Haznedar, C. Tang, J. Spiegel-Cohen, T. C. Wei, A. Solimando, et al. 2001. "Effect of Fluoxetine on

Regional Cerebral Metabolism in Autistic Spectrum Disorders: A Pilot Study." *International Journal of Neuropsychopharmacology* 4 (2):119–25.

Centers for Disease Control and Prevention (CDC). 2009. "Prevalence of Autism Spectrum Disorders—Autism and Developmental Disabilities Monitoring Network, United States, 2006." *Morbidity and Mortality Weekly Report* 58 (SS10):1–20.

———. 2011. "Autism Spectrum Disorders (ASDs): Data and Statistics." Accessed August 30. www.cdc.gov/ncbddd/autism/data.html.

Croen, L. A., D. V. Najjar, B. Fireman, and J. K. Grether. 2007. "Maternal and Paternal Age and Risk of Autism Spectrum Disorders." *Archives of Pediatrics and Adolescent Medicine* 161 (4):334–40.

Crooke, P. J., R. E. Hendrix, and J. Y. Rachman. 2008. "Brief Report: Measuring the Effectiveness of Teaching Social Thinking to Children with Asperger Syndrome (AS) and High Functioning Autism (HFA)." *Journal of Autism and Developmental Disorders* 38 (3):581–91.

Dawson, G., S. Rogers, J. Munson, M. Smith, J. Winter, J. Greenson, A. Donaldson, and J. Varley. 2010. "Randomized, Controlled Trial of an Intervention for Toddlers with Autism: The Early Start Denver Model." *Pediatrics* 125 (1):e17–23. doi:10.1542/peds.2009-0958.

Dawson, M., L. Mottron, and M. A. Gernsbacher. 2008. "Learning in Autism." In *Learning and Memory: A Comprehensive Reference*, edited by J. H. Byrne and H. Roediger, 759–72. New York: Elsevier.

Dawson, M., I. Soulières, M. A. Gernsbacher, and L. Mottron. 2007. "The Level and Nature of Autistic Intelligence." *Psychological Science* 18 (8):657–62.

Elder, L. M., J. Munson, A. M. Estes, B. King, and G. Dawson. 2009. "Patterns of Psychotropic Medication Use in Children with Autism Spectrum Disorders." Presentation at International Meeting for Autism Research (IMFAR), May 7, Chicago, IL.

Estes, A., J. Munson, G. Dawson, E. Koehler, X. H. Zhou, and R. Abbott. 2009. "Parenting Stress and Psychological Functioning among Mothers of Preschool Children with Autism and Developmental Delay." *Autism: International Journal of Research and Practice* 13 (4):375–87.

Feinstein, A. 2010. *A History of Autism: Conversations with the Pioneers.* West Sussex, UK: Wiley-Blackwell.

Flippin, M., S. Reszka, and L. R. Watson. 2010. "Effectiveness of the Picture Exchange Communication System (PECS) on Communication and Speech for Children with Autism Spectrum Disorders: A Meta-Analysis." *American Journal of Speech-Language Pathology* 19:178–95.

Freed, G. L., S. J. Clark, A. T. Butchart, D. C. Singer, and M. M. Davis. 2010. "Parental Vaccine Safety Concerns in 2009." *Pediatrics* 125 (4):654–59.

Freedman, B., L. Kalb, B. Zablotsky, and E. Stuart. 2010. "80 Percent Autism Divorce Rate Debunked in First-of-Its Kind Scientific Study." Kennedy Krieger Institute, May 19. Accessed May 26, 2011. http://www.kennedykrieger.org/overview/news/80-percent-autism-divorce-rate-debunked-first-its-kind-scientific-study.

Ganz, M. L. 2006. "The Costs of Autism." In *Understanding Autism: From Basic Neuroscience to Treatment,* edited by S. O. Moldin and J. L. R. Rubenstein, 474–502. Boca Raton, FL: CRC/Taylor and Francis.

———. 2007. "The Lifetime Distribution of the Incremental Societal Costs of Autism." *Archives of Pediatrics and Adolescent Medicine* 161 (4):343–49.

Geschwind, D. H. 2009. "Advances in Autism." *Annual Review of Medicine* 60:367–80.

Golan, O., and S. Baron-Cohen. 2006. "Systemizing Empathy: Teaching Adults with Asperger Syndrome or High-Functioning Autism to Recognize Complex Emotions using Interactive Multimedia." *Development and Psychopathology* 18 (2):591–617.

Gold, C., T. Wigram, and C. Elefant. 2006. "Music Therapy for Autistic Spectrum Disorder." *Cochrane Database of Systematic Reviews* 2, art. no. CD004381. doi:10.1002/14651858.CD004381.pub2.

Gordon, C. T., R. C. State, J. E. Nelson, S. D. Hamburger, and J. L. Rapoport. 1993. "A Double-Blind Comparison of Clomipramine, Desipramine, and Placebo in the Treatment of Autistic Disorder." *Archives of General Psychiatry* 50 (6):441–47.

Gould, E., J. Tarbox, D. O'Hora, S. Noone, and R. Bergstrom. 2011. "Teaching Children with Autism a Basic Component Skill of Perspective-Taking." *Behavioral Interventions* 26 (1):50–66.

Grandin, T. 2010. "The World Needs All Kinds of Minds." Presentation at ted.com, February. New York: TED Conferences, LLC. Accessed February 26. http://www.ted.com/talks/lang/en/temple_grandin_the _world_needs_all_kinds_of_minds.htm.

Greenspan, S. I., and S. Wieder. 2006. *Engaging Autism: Using the Floortime Approach to Help Children Relate, Communicate, and Think*. Cambridge, MA: Da Capo Press.

Grosso, K. 2011. "Do Couples Divorce Because of Autism? Parent Perceptions of Autism and Divorce." *Autism in Real Life* (blog), March 3. Accessed August 30. http://www.psychologytoday.com/blog/autism -in-real-life/201103/do-couples-divorce-because-autism.

Guastella, A. J., S. L. Einfeld, K. M. Gray, N. J. Rinehart, B. J. Tonge, T. J. Lambert, and I. B. Hickie. 2010. "Intranasal Oxytocin Improves Emotion Recognition for Youth with Autism Spectrum Disorders." *Biological Psychiatry* 67 (7):692–94.

Gutstein, S. E. 2009. *The RDI Book: Forging New Pathways for Autism, Asperger's, and PDD with the Relationship Development Intervention Program*. Houston, TX: Connections Center.

Hagerman, R. J., and P J. Hagerman, eds. 2002. *Fragile X Syndrome: Diagnosis, Treatment, and Research*. 3rd ed. Baltimore: Johns Hopkins University Press.

Hallmayer, J., S. Cleveland, A. Torres, J. Phillips, B. Cohen, T. Torigoe, J. Miller, et al. 2011. "Genetic Heritability and Shared Environmental Factors among Twin Pairs with Autism." *Archives of General Psychiatry* 68 (11):1095–1102. doi:10.1001/archgenpsychiatry.2011.76.

Harrison, J. E., and P. F. Bolton. 1997. "Annotation: Tuberous Sclerosis." *Journal of Child Psychology and Psychiatry* 38 (6):603–14.

Hartley, S. L., E. T. Barker, M. M. Seltzer, F. Floyd, J. Greenberg, G. Orsmond, and D. Bolt. 2010. "The Relative Risk and Timing of Divorce in Families of Children with an Autism Spectrum Disorder." *Journal of Family Psychology* 24 (4):449–57.

Hediger, M. L., L. J. England, C. A. Molloy, K. F. Yu, P. Manning-Courtney, and J. L. Mills. 2008. "Reduced Bone Cortical Thickness in Boys with Autism or Autism Spectrum Disorder." *Journal of Autism and Developmental Disorders* 38 (5):848–56.

Hertz-Piccotto, I. 2011. "Autism Now: Dr. Irva Hertz-Piccotto Extended Interview." *PBS NewsHour* (aired April 19). Accessed April 30. http://www.pbs.org/newshour/bb/health/jan-june11/piccottoext_04-19.html.

Hollander, E., A. Phillips, W. Chaplin, K. Zagursky, S. Novotny, S. Wasserman, and R. Iyengar. 2005. "A Placebo Controlled Crossover Trial of Liquid Fluoxetine on Repetitive Behaviors in Childhood and Adolescent Autism." *Neuropsychopharmacology* 30 (3):582–89.

Howard, J. S., C. R. Sparkman, H. G. Cohen, G. Green, and H. Stanislaw. 2005. "A Comparison of Intensive Behavior Analytic and Eclectic Treatments for Young Children with Autism." *Research in Developmental Disabilities* 26 (4):359–83.

Ibrahim, S. H., R. G. Voigt, S. K. Katusic, A. L. Weaver, and W. J. Barbaresi. 2009. "Incidence of Gastrointestinal Symptoms in Children with Autism: A Population-Based Study." *Pediatrics* 124 (2):680–86.

Immunization Safety Review Committee. 2004. *Immunization Safety Review: Vaccines and Autism.* Washington, DC: National Academies Press.

Interactive Autism Network (IAN). 2009. "IAN Research Report 9, May 2009: Family Stress Part 2: Work Life and Finances." Accessed August 30, 2011. http://iancommunity.org/cs/ian_research_reports/ian_research_report_may_2009.

Jaselskis, C. A., E. H. Cook Jr., K. E. Fletcher, and B. L. Leventhal. 1992. "Clonidine Treatment of Hyperactive and Impulsive Children with Autistic Disorder." *Journal of Clinical Psychopharmacology* 12 (5):322–27.

Kanner, L. 1943. "Autistic Disturbances of Affective Contact." *Nervous Child* 2:217–50. Reprint retrieved November 9, 2011. http://affect.media.mit.edu/Rgrads/Articles/pdfs/Kanner-1943-OrigPaper.pdf.

Kistner-Griffin, E., C. W. Brune, L. K. Davis, J. S. Sutcliffe, N. J. Cox, and E. H. Cook Jr. 2011. "Parent-of-Origin Effects of the Serotonin Transporter Gene Associated with Autism." *American Journal of Medical Genetics Part B: Neuropsychiatric Genetics* 156 (2):139–44.

Koegel, R. L., and L. K. Koegel. 2006. *Pivotal Response Treatment for Autism: Communication, Social, and Academic Development.* Baltimore: Paul H. Brookes.

Kogan, M. D., S. J. Blumberg, L. A. Schieve, C. A. Boyle, J. M. Perrin, R. M. Ghandour, G. K. Singh, B. B. Strickland, E. Trevathan, and P. C. van Dyck. 2009. "Prevalence of Parent-Reported Diagnosis of Autism Spectrum Disorder among Children in the US, 2007." *Pediatrics* 124 (5):1395–1403.

Lancet. 2010. "Retracted: Ileal-Lymphoid-Nodular Hyperplasia, Non-specific Colitis, and Pervasive Developmental Disorder in Children." 375 (9713):445.

Lang, R., L. K. Koegel, K. Ashbaugh, A. Regester, W. Ence, and W. Smith. 2010. "Physical Exercise and Individuals with Autism Spectrum Disorders: A Systematic Review." *Research in Autism Spectrum Disorders* 4 (4):565–76.

LeBlanc, L. A., A. M. Coates, S. Daneshvar, M. H. Charlop-Christy, C. Morris, and B. M. Lancaster. 2003. "Using Video Modeling and Reinforcement to Teach Perspective-Taking Skills to Children with Autism." *Journal of Applied Behavior Analysis* 36 (2):253–57.

Leyfer, O. T, S. E. Folstein, S. Bacalman, N. O. Davis, E. Dinh, J. Morgan, H. Tager-Flusberg, and J. E. Lainhart. 2006. "Comorbid Psychiatric Disorders in Children with Autism: Interview Development and Rates of Disorders." *Journal of Autism and Developmental Disorders* 36 (7):849–61.

Marcus, R. N., R. Owen, G. Manos, R. Mankoski, L. Kamen, R. D. McQuade, W. H. Carson, and R. L. Findling. 2011. "Safety and Tolerability of Aripiprazole for Irritability in Pediatric Patients with Autistic Disorder: A 52-week, Open-label, Multicenter Study." *Journal of Clinical Psychiatry.* 72 (9):1270-6.

Mariea, T. J., and G. L. Carlo. 2007. "Wireless Radiation in the Etiology and Treatment of Autism: Clinical Observations and Mechanisms." *Journal of the Australasian College of Nutritional and Environmental Medicine* 26 (2):3–7.

McDougle, C. J., L. E. Kresch, and D. J. Posey. 2000. "Repetitive Thoughts and Behavior in Pervasive Developmental Disorders: Treatment with

Serotonin Reuptake Inhibitors." *Journal of Autism and Developmental Disorders* 30 (5):427–35.

Mesibov, G. B., V. Shea, and E. Schopler. 2004. *The TEACHH Approach to Autism Spectrum Disorders.* New York: Springer Science+Business Media.

Mugno, D., L. Ruta, V. G. D'Arrigo, and L. Mazzone. 2007. "Impairment of Quality of Life in Parents of Children and Adolescents with Pervasive Developmental Disorder." *Health and Quality of Life Outcomes* 5:22–29.

Mukamel, Z., G. Konopka, E. Wexler, G. E. Osborn, H. Dong, M. Y. Bergman, P. Levitt, and D. H. Geschwind. 2011. "Regulation of MET by FOXP2, Genes Implicated in Higher Cognitive Dysfunction and Autism Risk." *Journal of Neuroscience* 31 (32):11437–42.

National Autism Center (NAC). 2011. *A Parent's Guide to Evidence-Based Practice and Autism: Providing Information and Resources for Families of Children with Autism Spectrum Disorders.* Randolph, MA: National Autism Center. Retrieved November 9. http://www.nationalautismcenter.org/pdf/nac_parent_manual.pdf.

National Institute of Neurological Disorders and Stroke (NINDS). 2011. "Tuberous Sclerosis Fact Sheet." Accessed October 30. http://www.ninds.nih.gov/disorders/tuberous_sclerosis/detail_tuberous_sclerosis.htm.

Notbohm, E. 2005. *Ten Things Every Child with Autism Wishes You Knew.* Arlington, TX: Future Horizons.

Ostovar, R. 2010. *The Ultimate Guide to Sensory Processing in Children: Easy, Everyday Solutions to Sensory Challenges.* Arlington, TX: Sensory World.

Park, J., M. Willmott, G. Vetuz, C. Toye, A. Kirley, Z. Hawi, K. J. Brookes, M. Gill, and L. Kent. 2010. "Evidence That Genetic Variation in the Oxytocin Receptor (OXTR) Gene Influences Social Cognition in ADHD." *Progress in Neuro-Psychopharmacology and Biological Psychiatry* 34 (4):697–702.

Posey, D. J., J. I. Putney, T. M. Sasher, D. L. Kem, and C. J. McDougle. 2004. "Guanfacine Treatment of Hyperactivity and Inattention in Pervasive Developmental Disorders: A Retrospective Analysis of 80 Cases." *Journal of Child and Adolescent Psychopharmacology* 14 (2):233–42.

Pottie, C. G., and K. M. Ingram. 2008. "Daily Stress, Coping, and Well-Being in Parents of Children with Autism: A Multilevel Modeling Approach." *Journal of Family Psychology* 22 (6):855–64.

Price, C. S., W. W. Thompson, B. Goodson, E. S. Weintraub, L. A. Croen, V. L. Hinrichsen, M. Marcy, et al. 2010. "Prenatal and Infant Exposure to Thimerosal from Vaccines and Immunoglobulins and Risk of Autism." *Pediatrics* 126 (4):656–64.

Prizant, B., A. Wetherby, E. Rubin, and A. Laurent. 2007. *The SCERTS Model.* Accessed 14 November 2011. www.scerts.com/index.php ?option=com_content&view=article&id=2Itemid=2.

Prizant, B. M., A. M. Wetherby, E. Rubin, A. C. Laurent, and P. J. Rydell. 2005. *The SCERTS Model: A Comprehensive Educational Approach for Children with Autism Spectrum Disorders.* Baltimore: Paul H. Brookes.

Quirmbach, L. M., A. J. Lincoln, M. J. Feinberg-Gizzo, B. R. Ingersoll, and S. M. Andrews. 2009. "Social Stories: Mechanisms of Effectiveness in Increasing Game Play Skills in Children Diagnosed with Autism Spectrum Disorder using a Pretest Posttest Repeated Measures Randomized Control Group Design." *Journal of Autism and Developmental Disorders* 39 (2):299–321.

Research Autism. 2011. "Alphabetic List of Autism Interventions, Treatments, and Therapies." Accessed July 27. http://www.research autism.net/alphabeticalinterventionlist.ikml.

Research Units on Pediatric Psychopharmacology (RUPP) Autism Network. 2002. "Risperidone in Children with Autism and Serious Behavioral Problems." *New England Journal of Medicine* 347 (5):314–21.

———. 2005. "Randomized, Controlled, Crossover Trial of Methylphenidate in Pervasive Developmental Disorders with Hyperactivity." *Archives of General Psychiatry* 62 (11):1266–74.

Rimland, B. 1964. *Infantile Autism: The Syndrome and Its Implications for a Neural Theory of Behavior.* New York: Appleton-Century-Crofts.

Rosenthal-Malek, A., and S. Mitchell. 1997. "Brief Report: The Effects of Exercise on the Self-Stimulatory Behaviors and Positive Responding of Adolescents with Autism." *Journal of Autism and Developmental Disorders* 27 (2):193–202.

Rossignol, D. A., L. W. Rossignol, S. Smith, C. Schneider, S. Logerquist, A. Usman, J. Neubrander, et al. 2009. "Hyperbaric Treatment for Children with Autism: A Multicenter, Randomized, Double-Blind, Controlled Trial." *BMC Pediatrics* 9:21.

Rudy, L. J. 2009. "Biomedical Treatments for Autism: About the Autism Research Institute and the DAN Protocol." *About.com*. Accessed March 30, 2010. http://autism.about.com/od/treatmentoptions/a/DANQand A.htm.

Sallows, G. O., and T. D Graupner. 2005. "Intensive Behavioral Treatment for Children with Autism: Four-Year Outcome and Predictors." *American Journal of Mental Retardation* 110 (6):417–38.

Scahill, L., M. G. Aman, C. J. McDougle, J. T. McCracken, E. Tierney, J. Dziura, L. E. Arnold, et al. 2006. "A Prospective Open Trial of Guanfacine in Children with Pervasive Developmental Disorders." *Journal of Child and Adolescent Psychopharmacology* 16 (5):589–98.

Singh, N. N., G. E. Lancioni, A. S. W. Winton, B. C. Fisher, R. G. Wahler, K. McAleavey, J. Singh, and M. Sabaawi. 2006. "Mindful Parenting Decreases Aggression, Noncompliance, and Self-Injury in Children with Autism." *Journal of Emotional and Behavioral Disorders* 14 (3):169–77.

Schieve, L. A., S. J. Blumberg, C. Rice, S. N. Visser, and C. Boyle. 2007. "The Relationship between Autism and Parenting Stress." *Pediatrics* 119 (Suppl. 1):S114–21.

Solomon, R., J. Necheles, C. Ferch, and D. Bruckman. 2007. "Pilot Study of a Parent Training Program for Young Children with Autism: The PLAY Project Home Consultation Program." *Autism* 11 (3):205–24.

Sussman, F. 1999. *More Than Words: Helping Parents Promote Communication and Social Skills in Children with Autism Spectrum Disorder.* Toronto, Canada: Hanen Centre.

Tiger, J. H., G. P. Hanley, and J. Bruzek. 2008. "Functional Communication Training: A Review and Practical Guide." *Behavior Analysis in Practice* 1 (1):16–23.

Vanderbilt Evidence-Based Practice Center. 2011. "Therapies for Children with Autism Spectrum Disorders." *Effective Health Care Program: Comparative Effectiveness Review* 26. Accessed August 30. http://effective

healthcare.ahrq.gov/ehc/products/106/656/CER26_Autism_Report
_04-14-2011.pdf.

Wakefield, A. J., S. H. Murch, A. Anthony, J. Linnell, D. M. Casson, M.
Malik, M. Berelowitz, et al. 1998. "Ileal-Lymphoid-Nodular Hyperplasia,
Non-specific Colitis, and Pervasive Developmental Disorder in
Children." *Lancet* 351 (9103):637–41.

Waldman, M., S. Nicholson, and N. Adilov. 2006. "Does Television Cause
Autism?" NBER Working Paper 12632, *The National Bureau of Economic
Research*, Cambridge, MA. http://nber.org/papers/w12632.

Weinstock, M. 2002. "Can the Behaviour Abnormalities Induced by
Gestational Stress in Rats Be Prevented or Reversed?" *Stress* 5
(3):167–76.

Welch, M. G. 2011. "Review: Secretin Is Not Effective for the Treatment
of Children with Autism Spectrum Disorders." *Evidence-Based Mental
Health* 14 (4):104.

Williams White, S., K. Keonig, and L. Scahill. 2007. "Social Skills
Development in Children with Autism Spectrum Disorders: A Review
of the Intervention Research." *Journal of Autism and Developmental Disorders*
37 (10):1858–68.

Wing, L., and J. Gould. 1979. "Severe Impairments of Social Interaction
and Associated Abnormalities in Children: Epidemiology and
Classification." *Journal of Autism and Developmental Disorders* 9 (1):11–29.

Zhang, J., and J. J. Wheeler. 2011. "A Meta-Analysis of Peer-Mediated
Interventions for Young Children with Autism Spectrum Disorders."
Education and Training in Autism and Developmental Disabilities 46
(1):62–77.

Anjali Sastry, PhD, is senior lecturer in system dynamics at the Massachusetts Institute of Technology Sloan School of Management and lecturer in the Department of Global Health and Social Medicine at Harvard Medical School. She investigates global health delivery and management, focusing on systems thinking and practical business-based approaches for increasing medical and prevention services in low-resource settings via numerous field studies in sub-Saharan Africa and South Asia. She serves on the boards of Management Sciences for Health and the Learning Project Elementary School. She, her husband, and their two sons, both of whom have been diagnosed on the autism spectrum, live in Brookline, MA.

Blaise Aguirre, MD, is an expert in child psychiatry including psychotherapy and psychopharmacology. He has worked extensively with children and their families and is an author and speaker on various aspects of mood, personality and development in children and adolescents. He is medical director of 3East at Harvard-affiliated McLean Hospital, a residential dialectical behavior therapy (DBT) program for young women exhibiting self-endangering behaviors and borderline personality traits. He has been a staff psychiatrist at McLean Hospital since 2000. He is an assistant professor of psychiatry at Harvard Medical School and lives in Lexington, MA, with his wife and their four children.

MORE BOOKS *from*
NEW HARBINGER PUBLICATIONS

**HELPING YOUR CHILD
WITH AUTISM SPECTRUM
DISORDER**

A Step-by-Step Workbook
for Families

ISBN: 978-1572243842 / US US $21.95
*Also available as an e-book
at newharbinger.com*

**HELPING YOUR CHILD
OVERCOME SEPARATION
ANXIETY OR
SCHOOL REFUSAL**

A Step-by-Step Guide for Parents

ISBN: 978-1572244313 / US $16.95
*Also available as an e-book
at newharbinger.com*

DON'T PICK ON ME

Help for Kids to Stand Up
to & Deal with Bullies

ISBN: 978-1572247130 / US $16.95
*Also available as an e-book
at newharbinger.com*
Instant Help Books
A Division of New Harbinger Publications, Inc.

**DON'T LET YOUR
EMOTIONS RUN YOUR
LIFE FOR TEENS**

Dialectical Behavior Therapy
Skills for Helping You Manage
Mood Swings, Control Angry
Outbursts & Get Along
with Others

ISBN: 978-1572248830 / US $16.95
*Also available as an e-book
at newharbinger.com*
Instant Help Books
A Division of New Harbinger Publications, Inc.

**THE RELAXATION &
STRESS REDUCTION
WORKBOOK FOR KIDS**

Help for Children to Cope with
Stress, Anxiety & Transitions

ISBN: 978-1572245822 / US $16.95
*Also available as an e-book
at newharbinger.com*
Instant Help Books
A Division of New Harbinger Publications, Inc.

I BET I WON'T FRET

A Workbook to Help Children
with Generalized
Anxiety Disorder

ISBN: 978-1572246003 / US $16.95
*Also available as an e-book
at newharbinger.com*
Instant Help Books
A Division of New Harbinger Publications, Inc.

newharbingerpublications, inc.
1-800-748-6273 / newharbinger.com

(VISA, MC, AMEX / prices subject to change without notice)

Like us on Facebook

Follow us on Twitter
@newharbinger.com

Don't miss out on new books in the subjects that interest you.
Sign up for our **Book Alerts** at newharbinger.com

ARE YOU SEEKING A CBT THERAPIST?

The Association for Behavioral & Cognitive Therapies (ABCT) Find-a-Therapist service offers
a list of therapists schooled in CBT techniques. Therapists listed are licensed professionals who
have met the membership requirements of ABCT & who have chosen to appear in the directory.

Please visit www.abct.org & click on *Find a Therapist*.